What People Are S

"Dr. Janet Mangum's book, *Until I See*, leads the reader into the vital spiritual dynamics that are essential for the parent or caregiver of a child with special needs. *Until I See* does a wonderful job of digging deep into the core values of the parent or caregiver. The book offers a rich environment of reflective writings, poems, prayers, and comforting thoughts that minister to the human spirit."

—Dr. Bill Peters, former Marine Corps officer, Co-Founder of the International Children's Aid Network

"Janet is one of those people who is out to change her world . . . whether leading teams into other nations, training and inspiring those under her leadership, or reaching out to the individual in need of a personal touch or word of encouragement. One of the groups that can so easily be overlooked is families with children having special needs. In her book, Janet offers support and strategies for families navigating what may be unchartered waters for them in the midst of emotional strain. Janet's goal in writing this book is that the heart of the caregiver—whether parent, relative, or friend—will be lifted up through the hope-filled stories, poems, and prayers she shares."

—Jane Hansen Hoyt, President/CEO Aglow International

"This is a 'must read' not only for those who discover they have special needs children but for everyone. Janet Mangum's engaging writing and powerful lessons of faith shared from real families are all laced with Scripture that will stir your heart and challenge your own personal walk with God. You too will become an overcomer. Read it and share these treasures with a friend."

—Apostle Dr. Naomi Dowdy, author, trainer, speaker, and former Senior Pastor at Trinity Christian Centre, Singapore

Until I See

Until I See

Peaceful Paths to Parenting Children With Special Needs

Melonie Janet Mangum

All stories in this book are real, but some of the names and identifying characteristics of individuals mentioned have been changed to protect their privacy. Professional therapists and counselors Carmenza Herrera Mendez, Michelle Phillips, Faith Raimer, Angela Timmons, Laurie Vervaecke, and Emily Zimbrich have graciously contributed portions of this book from their experiences.

Printed in the United States of America

For permission to use these materials, contact Janet Mangum at: makarismos@roadrunner.com or melonie.mangum@icloud.com.

ISBN: 1514290952
ISBN 13: 9781514290958

Dedication

This writing effort is dedicated to you, the reader. Whether it's been up close or a story from afar, many of you have been my teachers, counselors, and inspiration and some of you my heroes and heartfelt friends. Your stories have encouraged me to be a better person, trust our living Savior, and see beyond the immediate or natural into the heavenly, eternal realm. I am sure heaven's hosts are applauding your diligent dedication to your children as God's gift of life to be embraced and honored as you parent His precious ones.

Contents

Acknowledgments **xiii**
Introduction **xv**

Chapter 1 Sticker Shock: Who Am I?
Identity shock is often one of the beginning responses to the news that your child has some type of impairment. You find yourself in uncharted territory. Life is changing. Your values are challenged. You are figuring out who you are as you process through your new role. **1**

Chapter 2 Mighty Warrior: Why Me?
You know you are not equipped for the task at hand, and you begin to grapple with your own abilities or lack thereof. You find yourself feeling like the biblical character Gideon, stunned by a daunting commission and God's affirming declarations. **13**

Chapter 3 Transformation: Am I Melting?
There are typical stages in the transformation process: surviving, searching, settling, and separation. They become significant steps that keep you pressing forward with a healthy resolve. You are discovering the difference between your temporary, functional, and core identity. Your dynamic persona and purpose are strengthening your sense of capability. **25**

Chapter 4 The Zones: What Now?
Honing your skills as a parent of a child with special needs is laborious and exhausting. As you tap into that ability beyond your own, you uncover a capacity for courage and peace zones, a special grace of empowerment resident within your core identity in Christ Jesus. **39**

Chapter 5 Frozen Waterfalls: How Can I?
Emotions can create a sense of harsh, immobilizing cold. God's description of your persona and purpose and His gift of forgiveness are unlocking your heart, releasing you from guilt and shame. As you move forward, warmed by forgiveness toward yourself and others, His ice anchors are enabling you to climb. **55**

Chapter 6 Faith Lifts: What's Different?
You feel the difference. Something healthy is changing you on the inside. During the most unsettling times, you find yourself more relaxed, more poised. You have respites when it feels like you are resting in a cliff cabana or one of those brightly colored hanging cocoon chairs. **73**

Chapter 7 Elephant Sense: Where Do I Look?
Seemingly unrelated situations, things both said and done, are propelling you forward. It doesn't make sense at times, but the changes in you are working for your good and the good of your child. You are discovering provision where you never guessed it was possible. **87**

Chapter 8 Buttercups Under Ice: You Call This Progress?
Realistic perseverance, like the turtle and rabbit race, is beginning to pay off. The suffering is real, yet you find yourself humming a new song. In the midst of it all, your peace is increasing. You watch and wait for those small nuances of change, all the while inching toward the finish line. **103**

Chapter 9 Lion-Hearted Waiting: Can You Hear Me Roar?
Fainting at any bad news is just out. That's not you anymore (okay, maybe you're still moving toward it). No matter how many times you have to go through these situations, with each one you are becoming stronger, able to withstand even storms of hurricane proportions that might tempt to get you to give up. **119**

Chapter 10 Stalwart Seeds Grow Anywhere: Is It Spring Yet?
Comparisons can be your worst enemy, but who can resist them? Contentment in the midst of a maze of questions is transitioning your tears into a deeper level of wisdom. Rewarding. Worthwhile. A privilege. With an inward grin, you hear yourself repeating these words. You are more than redefined. You are being refined, and you are living the transformation. **133**

Chapter 11 Laughter of Grace: What Just Happened?
A merry heart is doing you good like a medicine. You and your child are finding the mystery of both the physical and emotional benefits of humor, laughter, and on occasion, joy indescribable. **151**

Chapter 12 Rest and Rejuvenate: Where's My Pillow?
You are beginning to wake up expecting God to have touched you while sleeping with renewed hope, vision, dreams, destiny, ideas, and direction. God's loving, personal presence welcomes you into what it means to come away and be with Him. **167**

Chapter 13 Trials, Triumphs & Connections: Can Miracles Happen?
Jesus turned water into wine in Cana at a wedding feast. He is turning the natural into a "God-infused natural" to the delight and surprise of everyone. As your perspective changes, you are discovering miraculous interventions you never knew existed. You are embracing a strong sense of expectancy for the future. **177**

Chapter 14 Finite Infinity—Limited Yet Unlimited!
Your life definitions are transforming. You have inherent, God-like spiritual DNA—God's family traits. You and your child are valuable to Him. You are His very own, even if no one in the family "flies just like the other birds." Your understanding of the purpose and value of life is exchanging with biblical and eternal perspectives. The limitation doors are blown away! **189**

Epilogue: A Trumpet Call of Prophetic Words **205**
Notes **209**
About the Author **213**

Acknowledgments

I am grateful to all the family, friends, ministry leaders, professionals, authors, writers, and the many others that added to the material herein. Many of them fit in several of the categories that follow. I am deeply thankful for everyone's heart and participation.

Family

My husband, Tom Mangum

Cordell Mangum, my son; Meredith Henderson, my daughter; and Vanessa and Tim Propersi, my daughter and son-in-law

My sister and brother-in-law, Carole and Russ Mangum

My niece, Roxanne Nilsen, and her husband, Ed

Ministry Leaders

Jana Comer, Lonnie Crowe, Naomi Dowdy, Gary Dunahoo, Cheryl Erbes, Susan Hafner, Fran Hallgren, Lana Heightley, Jane Hansen-Hoyt, Barbara Peters, Marnie Piuze

Counseling/Therapy Professionals

Carmen Herrera Mendez, Bill Peters, Michelle Phillips, Faith Raimer, Angela Timmons, Laurie Vervaeche, Emily Zimbrich

Authors

Nancy B. Miller, PhD, MSW, and insights in her book, *Nobody's Perfect*

Joni & Friends, and her speaking, blogs, and materials

Cindy Steinbeck author of *The Vine Speaks*

Melanie Boudreau, author of *Toppling the Idol of Ideal*

Contributing Writers

Jeff Andrus, Camille Block, Chuck Boudreau, Mark and Elaine Brown, Denette Dixon, Cheryl Erbes, Ron Lucarelli, Carol Martin, Justin Rice, and Sandra Yaroch

Others

Classroom special education teachers and para-professionals

Parents who sent their personal stories under pseudonyms

Parents at large who inspired me with their courage and dedication

The children and youth in schools where I served as a teacher's aide

Writers, musicians, and singers who gave me inspiration, including Leslie Mather, Ed and Roxanne Nilsen

Editor Karen Roberts, for her wise and loving heart and her faithful perseverance in the editing process

Introduction

I MARVEL AT how little ideas and steps are often the springboards to experiences I treasure. One of the most enriching experiences of my life, working with children with special needs and leading a support group for parents of these children, has become a springboard for me to create this book.

At the time, I had three school-age children and was going to school myself to finish my degrees. It would be ideal, I thought, if I could find a job that would allow me to be home when the children were out of school and leave time so that I could do my homework. Taking a position as a special education aide for the local school district seemed to answer those requirements.

What began with a day or two of filling in led to months on one assignment and then to a full year in another. Thus I began a journey that I thought would take only two years, but it extended and extended again. I had a sneaky feeling God was up to something more in my life.

I was quick to discover that these assignments required more energy than I originally expected. Still, as I began to watch the parents, I realized their level of ceaseless hard work and emotional stress seemed never ending in comparison to mine.

Personal Transformation

Life always looks easier from a distance, doesn't it? Most of us can learn and adapt to a new skill set when we choose, especially if it's simple and repetitive. My challenges requiring new skills were both external and internal, and I found the internal attitudes the most difficult to navigate. I had a choice. Was I going to turn off inside and get the job done on the outside, or would I fulfill my role from the inside out, with a God-perspective and God-provision?

In the journey, I found incredible encouragement and indescribable beauty. Now when I look back, I realize I can retitle the emotional and spiritual stories. Once they fell into the category of Duty and Disappointments; now the category is titled Royal Adventures. The story titles not only have transformed over time, but I have too. I am a different person than I was, grateful for the children, the parents, and God's intervention.

And Then

In my classroom, Kirk would have very difficult days. He would scream, pulling at his clothes, when his meds were off balance. Then before I knew it, if I turned my head the other way, Mary would have a mouth full of craft paste before I could stop her while Jerry stood terrified in the corner for who knows what reason this time! These scenarios and more were repeated over and over. They weighed heavily on body, mind, and spirit.

When I was on assignment as an aide for a year, I was one of three adults who carried on with the myriad of additional and necessary burdens due to the school administration's battle with budget cuts. At first I was shocked at the amount of "giving" required and amazed at how gracefully my two colleagues met every challenge. Even so, we clearly had days when the intense concentration and outpouring of energy took their toll.

One morning at break I had to be addressed three times before a colleague could get my attention. I was off in another world, soaked in mental perspiration from the intense time we had just had in class and trying to marshal my resolve to face what would be coming in ten short minutes. At the close of that school day, I was at the end of my resources. I stood on the school lawn with a thousand-yard stare, watching the children board their bus. If I was thinking at all, it was about getting myself home. On a scale of 1 to 10, zeal could barely be counted. Zero. Well, maybe zero plus ½.

That moment was when a God-idea struck. Unexpectedly I began to wonder about the parents who would hug those kids once they got home. My guess was that none of the parents had degrees in nursing or education. They did not get a paycheck for taking care of their own flesh and blood. If they retired to a friendly sofa in the evening to kick off their shoes and forget about the events of the day, they probably couldn't ever fully relax with the assumption that their young ones would lie peacefully in bed all through the night.

Hard labor in a classroom was one thing. What was it like at home? I assumed home must have a variety of struggles: potential grim disappointments, nagging fears, frequent doctor visits and negative reports, near constant frustration, and more than likely family strife. Suddenly I was pierced through the heart with compassion. What was overwhelming to me in that moment was that the parents' job went on unceasingly, for days and nights on end, for weeks, months, and years that stretched into a vast uncertainty. Even when days were punctuated with laughter, charm, and warmth, how could they not feel wounded, abandoned, anxiety ridden, and sometimes completely depleted?

As I ached inside at the levels of sacrifice and challenge those parents had to go to, I found myself thinking, *Someone who doesn't have a child with special needs should do something for them.*

Answered Prayer

That evening I began a new prayer focus, searching for what I could do. I had worked with children who ranged in age from two years to eighteen years, children who had a wide variety of physical and emotional problems being dealt with both at the school district and at the local mental hospital. I was not convinced that I could find a way to engender grace-empowered peace.

As I continued listening and praying, my more immediate desire became what was needed in the interim, in the moments of each daily routine. In that moment of insight, it was as if I were in the private prayer time of one those parents. I found myself praying *with* them as well as *for* them:

> *"Heavenly Father, until I see You face to face or in the answer that I seek, may I be found in Your abiding grace, my soul quieted by Your peace."*

I had my answer, or at least part of it—abiding grace and peace. Which of us, regardless of the health of our children, doesn't need more grace and peace? Perhaps I could somehow offer a time of refreshing that would promote an overriding experience saturated by these God-empowered virtues.

Direction

The group I wanted to gather would include parents and caregivers who came from different faith traditions. All good things, I believed, came from God's extravagant love and unparalleled wisdom. They included any benefit from art and science, the latest advancements in medicine, as well as many wellness models of psychology. There were so many directions I could go. I was open to all good things. Which way should I choose?

And there was my impasse. My experience was teaching in special education classes. I had one moderate ADHD child of my own. I doubted those experiences alone qualified me. I wasn't a therapist or doctor, so I was concerned that my lack of education in practical psychology would impair the effectiveness of the group gathering and my ability to facilitate these sessions.

A Kid to the Rescue

My dream began to fizzle. What was I thinking? Then one morning, my student assignment, Ryan, rushed up to me in class. "Mrs. Mangum! I'm in a book!" His face was lit up like a Christmas tree as he thrust a brochure into my hands. It advertised a book entitled *Nobody's Perfect* by Nancy Miller, a doctor of psychology who taught at UCLA at the time.

I bought the book and gobbled up its insights into the world of parents of children with special needs. It wasn't a book you would find on a religious shelf in the library because of its approach. As I read through it, the concepts brought parental validation alongside practical application. Now I had the perfect adjunct to the group, and I was once again on fire to start. With *Nobody's*

Perfect as the springboard, I was confident I could offer a safe, nourishing time together.

Once the group started and began to thrive, the book's author, Dr. Miller, and Joni Eareckson Tada from Joni and Friends worldwide ministry, both graciously gave up a Saturday to speak at a daylong seminar for us. Afterwards, Dr. Miller and I exchanged ideas for collaboration, and she encouraged me to take the idea of a book further. Time and life took precedence until now, but these pages would not exist without Ryan's inspiration and Dr. Miller and Joni Eareckson Tada's encouragement in that first group.

The Good Fight

The parents who chose to be part of the group gathered weekly to comfort one another, to exchange ideas, to network about services they had discovered, and to engage in God's loving perspectives on their circumstances. As I had hoped, they came from diverse backgrounds; their children had a range of needs; but none of their differences mattered. They were united in sharing what they had of themselves. Their hard work, endurance, and caring ways demonstrated tremendous strength of character. From my perspective, they could have run a nation honorably if given the chance, but instead their lives were being poured out for the sake of their children.

They sought peace to refresh their souls and grace to keep focused and effective. They struggled at times to maintain their positive focus; yet they kept extending themselves until God's grace and supernatural, grace-enabled peace began to be tangibly felt. When some were aching from the raw suffering, hearing stories of how their newfound grace and peace overflowed into their families and those around them kept us all hopeful.

My prayer was that their influence would go far beyond what they might have imagined possible. I also prayed that what they inspired in me would someday be able to point disappointed and work-ravaged souls to find healing in the "peace of God which transcends all understanding" offered by the multiplied grace and peace of Jesus Christ (Philippians 4:7; 1 Corinthians 1:3; 2 Peter 1:2).

Core Values

As I journeyed with the group, I realized that parents of children with special needs often deal with defining core values. They consciously or subconsciously search for a point system that determines a person's worth in a family and in society. Some repeatedly struggle with their personal sense of ability in their new, functional identity. Others face being overwhelmed with multiple identity complexities over and above static realities like each of us is human or each is a daughter or a son.

When a traumatic event occurs or a condition is diagnosed, I learned that personal identity branding with the past identity markers may go into a tailspin or be temporarily immobilized by the shock. Sooner or later the parents of these children with special needs would ask questions like "Who am I now?" and "How do I describe myself?" and "How do others describe me?" and "How do I process these changes?"

This Book

This book is meant to encourage parents and caregivers dealing with challenging core value shifts due to the situations and conditions in their child's life. The personal stories interjected may be from people walking a different path than your own; yet they may lift you in your journey, strengthen your convictions, validate your longings, and energize your spirit while you are processing daily life and parenting through your child's mental or physical impairment or disease.

Included in this book are writings by therapist Faith A. Raimer, Licensed Marriage, Family and Child Therapist, life coach, speaker, and author who holds an MA in marriage, family, and child therapy and a BA in psychology and business. I am grateful for her contributions as well as friendship and wisdom as she read through this material and provided input from her vast experience. Also included are insights from counselor Carmenza Herrera Mendez, who is a bilingual speech and language therapist with over fifteen years in clinical pediatric practice in Colombia and Singapore. She is the founder and director of "habilmente" a private pediatric therapy center for children in Columbia.

Valuable contributions also are included from counselor Michelle Phillips, Licensed Marriage and Family Therapist and Nationally Certified School

Psychologist; counselor Angela Timmons, DPA, LCSW, California State University Channel Islands, also a musician and speaker; Rev. Dr. Laurie Vervaecke, LCPC, LCCC, Licensed Clinical Pastoral Counselor and Licensed Clinical Christian Counselor; and counselor Emily Zimbrich, Licensed Professional Counselor (LPC) and Chemical Dependency Counselor Supervisor (CDCS).

A special feature of this book is the end-of-chapter interactive material. The PRAY section gives sample words you might voice to God in response to the thoughts presented in the chapter. I encourage you to use them to begin a prayer with God and see where you own words lead you. The REFLECT section offers several prompts to help you process, in concrete ways specific to your life, what you have read and thought about in the chapter as you read it. I encourage you to accept the challenge of interacting with at least one REFLECT option in each chapter. You may choose to journal your thoughts as you do.

Because the interactive material at the end of the chapters could require considerable time and effort on your part, you may desire to read only one chapter a week.

Finally, though not least in importance, I have interspersed in each chapter my reflective writings: poems and prayers and comforting thoughts such as the one that follows.

Finite Infinity

I had a glimpse of faith
Saw something of charity,
Heard with absolute clarity
Several words of hope
From others I assumed were
Better than I at running this race.
Then one seemed to falter,
And I heard myself offer,
“Okay, I’ll walk with you a bit.”
In response I got a look that said
I must be bursting with His grace.

1

Sticker Shock: Who Am I?

Shock, worry, frustration, and fear—natural reactions—soon to be superseded by new expressions of a positive reality and honoring identity

WE ALL HAVE experienced sticker shock at one time or another. Whether it is the price of a new television or the long awaited home, when it hits, we are stunned by the cost. Identity shock is much like sticker shock.

Identity as a parent of a child with special needs has its own kind of sticker shock responses. Initial reactions may be "Me, now, why?" and "You've got to be kidding." Major questions may follow such as, "How much more costly is it going to get emotionally and financially? How much more stress can my marriage endure? What about the time demands? What about my career? Am I going to be able to pay the price?" The questions change quickly from "Who am I now?" ones to "Who will I have to become as a parent of a child with special needs?" As you read this book, you have probably already experienced some identity shifting.

IDENTITY SHIFT: Life Is Changing

Gloria tells about the first time in her parental role encountering the sticker shock of being the parent of a child with special needs. As she pushed her grocery cart down the aisle with her small child inside, an incredulous shopper leaned over and whispered to her, "Oh my! You must have committed a crime in the past or done something awful to cause your child to be so afflicted." Stunned to the core, Gloria was too shocked even to respond to such an incredible level of cruelty. She pushed on in an attempt to finish her shopping.

Unfortunately parents of children with special needs do encounter insensitive people, clueless in the moment, people who seem to have an innate need to label what they don't understand. Thankfully God holds a far higher value to our identity. He holds the key to our developing process, which is the power of transformation.

Luke 10:25–37

Fear, fear,
what do they fear?
The very need
that drew them near.

Help them see Jesus,
His eyes, His heart.
Help them see Jesus,
His love impart.

Then whether or not
they know what to do,
when they see Jesus,
His mercy shines through.

IDENTITY REEVALUATION: Keeping a Healthy Focus

What if a couple were advised to purchase a piece of expensive business property with the expectation that it was going to generate tremendous future profit, and then in a year, the whole deal fell through? Their dream, it seemed, turned out to be nothing but hard work with little personal gain. How would they feel? Frustrated, stunned, angry, maybe embarrassed, and certainly cheated!

The tropical vacation they had their hearts set on when the property started turning a large profit was no longer possible. They longingly looked back over the brochures. It was to have been on a French-speaking island. They had gone so far as to learn some of the language, but now the trip had to be canceled.

Then a friend who understood their disappointment offered them a gift to take its place, an Alaskan cruise with an inland geologic rock adventure. Accepting this generous gift would require a major adjustment with a drastic change of plans. Time for a reality check.

First things first. They reevaluate their situation. They make a herculean effort to keep a healthy perspective. They focus on the positive. It can't be that bad, right? They look back over the cruise's many excellent promises of delicious food, entertainment, and scenery. Traveling with a group of "rock hounds" could be intellectually stimulating. Maybe they will see a rare treasure and discover the personal transformation that is waiting for them on that ship to Alaska. While they are foraging for rock treasures, they might just find an undiscovered beauty of nature. They could even come across some shimmering gold deposits in their natural setting. It is an unexpected gift, an opportunity to widen their horizons when they choose to make the most of it.

This evaluation process can be similar to what parents experience after the initial sticker shock when they first discover that they are parents of a child with special needs. The impending circumstances call for clear thinking, patience, and love for themselves and their child and demand critical decisions while they are still in shock. There is no time to sit and ponder options. They must make choices without the benefit of the due diligence they would normally rely on.

What has changed for these parents now? They are certainly not the eager French-speaking tourists dressed in tropical attire, warming themselves somewhere in the sun. As the parents of a child with special needs, they must accept a new identity in all aspects of their life. How will this new identity affect daily routines, and how will it affect the overall quality of family life? How can they be expected to process all the new feelings while in a constant state of pressure and varying levels of disbelief and pain? It is important to breathe deeply, smile inwardly when possible, refocus, and get on board with a decision to trust God in the journey!

Prayer for Grace in Challenges

Dear heavenly Father, what was is no more. And what is required is so much more. Immerse me in Your equipping love, and outfit me for new challenges ahead. I choose to trust Your definition of who I am and Your transforming grace in who I am becoming. In Jesus' precious Name, I believe; help my unbelief. I choose to rely on the power of Your Holy Spirit. I receive Your enabling grace.

TREASURE HUNTING

Thankfully for most parents of children with special qualities, a positive transformation of their identity emerges soon out of the transition time. Although possibly unwanted at first, the new identity and its value system can become a privileged badge of honor. They uncover treasure as their values take on new dimensions. They find themselves loving what they didn't even know existed a few weeks or months ago. They enjoy what they never dreamed they would spend time doing. The revelation of a deeper relationship with their heavenly Father is precious, and the thought begins to dawn on them that it can be transfiguring.

The self-discoveries, some of them defined and refined by the child's unique needs, are usually overwhelming. Parents discover that they too have caverns of special needs. Along the way, as they find those respites of God's stabilizing peace, the journey becomes transformational and affirms their determination and dedication.

Roxanne and Ed share a gripping account of their journey from what they considered a normal life into their personal identity shock in a matter of weeks.

Our Life as It Should Be?

We were expecting our first baby, we both had great jobs, and we owned our first condo.

I was due the first of September and was fully planning on teaching right after delivery. But then the twist. I had an extremely difficult delivery and postpartum hemorrhage, and I had to be hospitalized for a week before coming home with our son. Doctor's orders kept me from returning to school for six weeks.

About the six-week mark, as I was getting ready to return to work, I decided to take our son, Drew, to the pediatrician for his six-week well check. Mind you, we also had gone in for the two-week well check, and he had checked out just fine.

This time the pediatrician was very quiet during the exam. She asked several questions and then left the room. After what seemed like forever, she returned with a very solemn expression and said, "Your baby is in heart failure. You need to see a specialist right away."

At the time, I didn't understand fully what that meant. Heart failure? Did she mean heart attack? I couldn't think. I couldn't speak. I asked whom to call, and she said she had already called and the doctor was expecting me. She warned me to drive safely. Drive safely, right! I couldn't even push the button on the elevator to get to the parking garage.

When I finally gained a little composure and got downstairs, I called my husband. And then somehow I got to the doctor's office, a pediatric cardiologist, and waited for the next exam, all the while checking my baby to make he was still breathing.

> You might say, "Six weeks, how could you not know that something was wrong with your baby for six weeks?" During that time I was very weak and still recovering. I had contracted a bacterial infection and had to be rehospitalized. In the meantime, I continued nursing our little boy. He was gaining weight and sleeping and doing all things little babies do without any trouble.
>
> In spite of all the right signals of a healthy baby coming my way, I was about to learn that PDA, or Patent Ductus Arteriosis, had made its way into my son. It is a condition in which the duct that is open in vitro for the mother and child to share oxygenated blood remains open after birth. It typically closes soon after birth; however, in our son's case, his remained open.
>
> It was after the intense surgery and while our son was fighting for his life, accompanied by a life support system, that we learned the whole truth concerning his condition. Our son had been born with multiple heart defects.

As you might suspect, a laundry list of fear, anger, emotional pain, and extreme negativity accompanied by sheer exhaustion struck Roxanne and Ed Nilsen like a freight train headed down a hill.

Roxanne continued to process her new identity. "I thought, *God, why him? Why us? I didn't drink one diet soda and did everything right during pregnancy. Did I leave out some crucial vitamin? Could my child's condition have been in the family line DNA?* I have to admit, I had some ungodly questions like, 'Why us and not some high-schooler and his girlfriend who got pregnant? Why not that person who just had what we always considered a normal baby but was on drugs her entire pregnancy? Hadn't we been following Christ as we should?'"

She and Ed had drastic, game-changer moments, days, and years ahead of them. They already had a strong connection and relationship with the Spirit of God, and eventually they came into peace with their vital role in the life of their child. As they discovered over the years, whether emotions validate this truth or not, it's an honor to be entrusted with children, any children—to be a parent.

Roxanne and Ed knew that God had given them Drew to be their son. They were able to experience the joy and honor of being his parents. With Drew they shared many a belly roll of laughter alongside a stream of loving, treasured encounters.

"God knew our future," Roxanne said. "In time we accepted our parenting circumstances and began to uncover skills and strengths we never knew we had. Our son would never fully recover. His life was short, but we clung to Proverbs 3:5–6 (NLT), "Trust in the LORD with all your heart; do not depend on your own understanding. Seek his will in all you do, and he will show you which path to take."

As gifted musicians, Roxanne and Ed were able to include their journey in several of their songs that speak of God's provision during difficult times and of their deep love of their son, Drew.

As Long As I'm Here

by Roxanne and Ed Nilsen (used by permission)

(Chorus)
I will sing as long as I'm here
of the love that breaks through the tears
of the day that I hope I see
when your eyes are looking at me . . .

Therapist Faith Raimer shares her insights on identity shock.

From Numb to a New Norm

Shock is the result of an unexpected jolt or surprise that jars the human system: body and mind. Alarmed and armed, the brain signals for an immediate discharge of electricity to stimulate nerves and muscles to prepare for action. In the animal world that physical response basically means one of two reactions: fight or flight. A grizzly seeing another bear moving in on his special, salmon-stocked site will act to conquer or concede.

The fight or flight reaction is innate in humans too, but unlike animals, we have been given an even greater ability to consider all options before making a reasonable decision. Ordinarily we can look before we leap. Not so with shock. When life throws us a curve ball, we are caught off guard and can become stunned into numbness, unable to respond. The mind isn't immediately adjusting to something so unthinkable. Instead it reacts to the new reality with disbelief, a mental rejection of what is true. This reaction is neither unusual nor unhealthy—as long as it is temporary.

The key for you to be able to move from numb to your definition of normal is acceptance. Acceptance may or may not indicate approval, but it does allow a bridge to be established between your reality and your preferred perception of it. You are then better able to take the next steps.

Clients of mine have found a phrase I coined to be helpful in these times: "I can manage even that which I cannot control." It has worked for me as well on more than one occasion. It means we can't always control our circumstances, but we can manage how we deal with them. That, too, is a useful key.

Another key is to think in terms of "up until now." Up until now, I was anxious and afraid. Up until now, I was confused and considered myself inadequate. Saying statements such as these allows you to recognize what you believe to be true for the moment. At the same time, it clears a path for change. You can mindfully create a positive shift to whatever is better for you, starting now.

These keys have proven useful over and again in helping to cope and affect positive change, but there is an even greater tool that is yours for the asking. This key is a gift from God that can take you above and beyond your current condition. It can help you open doors that up until now were closed or locked. It can also guide you through them from this point to reward. God's key is His loving gift of grace that helps you open up to His perspective, even in times that seem uncertain or impossible. "The Lord is near. Do not be anxious about anything, but in everything, by prayer and petition, with thanksgiving, present your requests to God. And the peace of God, which transcends all understanding, will guard your hearts and your minds in Christ Jesus" (Philippians 4:5b–7).

How reassuring it is to know God wants to guard your heart and mind for now, all time, and beyond. Only God can. Only God. Call out His Name, "Jesus." Whisper it, say it aloud or silently, repeating it until your inner peace is restored. He waits at your door. Will you open it to Him?

TREASURES: Nature's Declaration

Heaven and earth declare God's glory and reveal hidden beauty (Psalm 19:1). Take a peek at Alaska's glaciers, the majestic redwoods in northern California, the consistency of the ocean waves coming in and going out day after day at your favorite beach setting, or the extravagant detail of the nearby flora. Look for the hints of His marvelous handiwork in the heavens as well—the sunrises, sunsets, and starry nights. As you take time to reflect on the marvels of nature, you will find yourself inspired and in awe of God's transforming work.

When you gaze at His treasures, His thoughts can become your own. His character will show up in you when you least expect it, and His love will surprise your own emotional ability to love. His comfort releases spectacular moments as hints of joy surface in your life again.

The Scriptures Jesus quoted about Himself from the Old Testament in Isaiah 61:1–3 become your personal testimony of His spectacular love: "The Spirit of the Sovereign LORD is on me, because the LORD has anointed me to proclaim good news to the poor. He has sent me to bind up the brokenhearted, to proclaim freedom for the captives and release from darkness for the prisoners, to proclaim the year of the LORD's favor and the day of vengeance of our God, to comfort all who mourn, and provide for those who grieve in Zion—to bestow on them a crown of beauty instead of ashes, the oil of joy instead of mourning, and a garment of praise instead of a spirit of despair. They will be called oaks of righteousness, a planting of the LORD for the display of his splendor."

Dramatic beauty and displays of His splendor also hide in drab, rough, outwardly unattractive, and seemingly ordinary rocks. Some, when broken open, reveal incredible crystal formations—rainbows of colors, surprising treasures hidden inside by God's amazing, natural processes. Who knew that looking inside rocks could be such adventure?

Hard circumstances, like rocks, contain the potential for spectacular, colorful, crystal moments. God wants to create miracles of beauty in us in impossible places.

RARE BEAUTY

Take a lesson from geologists as they search through nature's history. From their slow, laborious task unfolds an artful mystery. The intriguing matter of the bedrock on which we stand transforms their tedious labor on a quest for data into a royal adventure where amazing, sparkling discoveries are made.

Geologists are explorers of nature's brilliant beauty, even in its humblest creations. Most of the rest of us, on the other hand, are casual observers with far greater limitations. We don't have the tools to dig deep in the earth or to open what may look like ordinary rocks on the outside to see the beauty hidden within.

No museum of art could match the dazzling color and abstract shapes that rocks display. Oh, if we could only remember to see each other that way.

PRAY

Heavenly Father, Lord Jesus, I desire to be a treasure hunter, a parental geologist in Your kingdom of love here on earth. Enlighten me in my true identity as a child of God, a person of character, and a valuable, life-giving parent. Enable me to be willing to do the necessary work. Awaken and empower my identity in transition. Help me find peace in Your enlightened, transfiguring process. Reveal the eternal worth of both my child and me. I want to understand Your perspective of the value of our lives, not as people see and judge, but as only You can—*with heaven's eyes!*

REFLECT

1. As a parent of a child with special needs, you have identified yourself already in certain ways. You have the choice to take on or reject further aspects of your new identity that come from the comments and reactions of others to define or label you. If, for example, you are pushing a wheelchair and someone opens a door for you, you are being identified by the one opening the door for you as someone deserving courtesy. You may already have experienced other, greater expressions of respect, admiration, kindness, and love. Can you name some of them? These are the warming, positive identities that only someone in your place is privileged to know and enjoy.

2. Take a moment to think of something beautiful you saw or heard recently that impressed you. Reflect on its beauty. Breathe deeply. Let it become a shining, crystal moment—a gift from God to you. What message could it give to you about who you are in God's eyes?

2

Mighty Warrior: Why Me?

Fear, denial, blame, and overwhelmed
to evolving hope and willingness

THE TRANSFORMING PROCESS is moving you from weak, overwrought, confused, and fearful to strong, confident, clear, and bold. You are becoming a mighty warrior, able to face the challenges, even as you process the "why me."

Janice's friends thought she could do it. Her family agreed. She didn't. Her bounce-back response to their encouraging words was the same incredulous thought, a sometimes inaudible shout, "Why me? I am not trained, skilled, or experienced! This hasn't ever been me nor will it ever be! Bottom line: I'm no hero. I can't do this."

> "I can relate to Gideon's story in the book of Judges," Janice grimaced before sharing insights on her personal 20-year journey as a mom of two children with vastly different special needs."
>
> "Before Gideon has his redefining encounter with God's angel, the story describes him as clueless, fearful, and trying to hide from the impending problems. He thinks he knows who he is and what God will do, which is nothing. Then comes the shock. God not only calls him by name but also redefines his persona (his perceived character) and purpose by addressing him as 'mighty warrior' (Judges 6:12)."

UNLIKELY HERO

The Bible's book of Judges tells the history of God's treasured nation from the time the people entered into the Promised Land, after their exodus from slavery in Egypt, to the rise of the monarchy approximately five centuries later. The list of judges before the first king is anointed is a long one, and all of those leaders are flawed, some more than others.

The Lord, of course, is the ultimate merciful and loving Judge. He allows His chosen people to do as they choose. In consequence of their choosing to turn away from Him, marauders from the east "like swarms of locusts" raid villages, plunder livestock and crops, and force the people to hide in caves "until they cried out to the LORD for help" (Judges 6: 5–6).

God mercifully delivers them by giving them a new judge. He chooses Gideon, a young man who has been working in a winepress where he threshes a bit of wheat harvested from a clandestine field, minding his own business and trying to keep out of sight of the raiding parties. Ultimately Gideon cuts a dashing figure in battle, but his first reactions to God's call on his life are doubt, fear, and an overwhelming identity crisis.

Gideon begins by denying the Lord's charge defining him as a mighty warrior. He reminds God that his family is the weakest in the nation, and he is the least in his family. He is not just being modest. He is completely overwhelmed by his self-evaluation. (Does that sound familiar?)

To his credit, Gideon is honest about his doubts. When an angel appears to him, declaring, "The LORD is with you, mighty warrior" (v. 12), how did Gideon respond? Does he rise up with immediate courage and say, "Wow, an angel! That settles it. God is with me! I can't miss. Yahoo, I'm ready. Let's go." Not even close.

Instead Gideon politely points out the upsetting current problem and the fact that it hadn't looked to him like God was with his family or his people for quite a while. "But," Gideon replies to the angel, "If the LORD is with us, why has all this happened to us?" His erroneous conclusion? The Lord had abandoned him and his people.

Who wouldn't react like Gideon? The problems were beyond his ability to overcome. If God was looking at him to make the difference, all he could imagine was imminent defeat. The future looked bleak, and he was being told he's the mighty warrior that can make the difference. Yeah, right!

Gideon was struggling. You struggle too. It's understandable that while you are about the business of parenting in your new identity, you long for some clear direction. So did Gideon, who could see no clear path ahead. You have an important role to fill, and you want to make sure what you are doing is what's best for everyone. Gideon came face to face with a significant choice. Was he going to believe God about who he could become or his own past? Like Gideon, you face an angel's message and a choice.

Surviving. That's the best Gideon could do until the Lord empowered and transformed him for the next stages of his life. What about you?

SURVIVING

Nancy Miller in her book, *Nobody's Perfect,* describes four stages that parents of special needs children go through. You may recognize them in your life with the particulars unique to your specific circumstances.

- *Surviving*
- *Searching*
- *Settling*
- *Separating*

Behind her four words is practical wisdom for the situations you might be struggling to understand. As you begin to grapple with the emotional input at each of these stages, you ready yourself for some transitional identity transformations.

Like Gideon, parents of children with special needs are in need themselves. They need reassurances for their battles. Someone's true story is encouraging when it declares, "I survived and you can too."

Terry, a pilot for many years, said the surviving stage for him was all about cause and effect. He felt like there were no answers, just daily trying to deal with emergency stress.

In flying, when a pilot is under emergency stress, the eyesight changes, the hearing changes. This and other physiological changes are to be expected. Previous repetitive training in the basics is critical in knowing how to manage when it happens. Intense focus is required. Keeping those wings straight and level on the altitude horizon indicator is the main focus—intense focus.

Terry didn't find the emergency stress of flying to be much different as a dad of a child with special needs. His pilot training helped him focus while transitioning from one stage to another. And yes, he made a safe landing.

Another dad stated that the surviving stage for him had few if any adequate answers. "It feels," he said, "like you are on the practice court with a racquetball machine set to a return speed far beyond your reflex capability. You're swinging at everything, sweating profusely. Balls are flying off the walls in every direction. Your inward mantra screams, 'Just keep your eye on that next ball coming at you.'"

After Gideon's initial response to the angel's words, he begins his transition from the *surviving* stage to the *searching* stage. At the same time, he extends himself as best he can and struggles (swings at a few racquet balls). And he doesn't stop pressing into the reality of his new, God-initiated identity and destiny.

Surviving. It starts with the reality of learning that your child is impaired, handicapped, or disabled mentally or physically. There may be denial. Usually is. Must be wrong. Must be a fix out there somewhere.

Remember those gut-wrenching minutes, hours, and days (maybe years) when you felt out of control? What were those times like for you? Mighty warrior or mighty worrier? Was there anger and bargaining with God? So-what's-He-going-to-do-about-your-situation thoughts?

The Lord's answer to Gideon can be applied to any of His overwhelmed family. Yes, you! "Go with the strength you have. . . . I am sending you!" (Judges 6:14 NLT).

Active, take-charge parents are particularly vulnerable to feeling helpless. And it doesn't take long before everyone is exhausted. Triumphs at the survival stage can often be reduced to one goal: making it through the day.

In the end, history reports Gideon as a transformed hero of faith. He wasn't without his doubts and fears along the way, but he learned to rely on God's identity definition for him rather than his own, limited one. In other words, Gideon was a mighty warrior before he had any idea who he could be or what he could accomplish.

Your heavenly Father wants all of His family to partake in the mystery of the ages. His exquisite, defining purpose is to bring each one into His secret wisdom, a wisdom that has been hidden and yet now is ready to be revealed in you and through you (1 Corinthians 2:7). His ultimate goal is to transform you, "rename you," to return you to your true identity. He means to fill you with His glorious nature, with abundant resources of His goodness and grace.

It's your opportunity to consider God's identity definition of your role as a parent of a child with special needs. You are in the process of your identity transformation. In it you will discover an uplifting persona and purpose beyond your imagination. You are emerging. You too are a warrior in and with His surpassing grace. Would you consider bravely saying it out loud before you are fully convinced? Say your name in the blank space here. "I, ________________________ (first and last name), am becoming a mighty warrior!"

AUTOPILOT

Elaine Brown recalls surviving on autopilot.

Surviving on Autopilot

I can still recall the day we brought our son, Matt, into the doctors' office for a physical examination. He was 4 1/2 at the time. Matt was in special education classes due to speech delay. His teacher noticed that he was having a difficult time riding a tricycle.

It was about 2 weeks later that the pediatrician gave us a call and asked if he could come by the house. Big red flag went up. What doctor makes house calls? My husband and I were sitting in the living room with the doctor while he proceeded to explain to us that Matthew had Duchenne's muscular dystrophy. He was 90 percent certain but wanted us to go to a neurologist and to have a biopsy done on his muscles.

> I really don't know how to describe how I felt at that moment. At that time, the medical field really didn't know much about Duchenne's except that it affected males only and that it usually was passed on by the mother. In our case I was not a carrier, there was no history in the family, and my mother came from a family of six girls. So the medical field said then it was a mutated gene, which could happen in 10 percent of the cases.
>
> Wow, so now what? Matt weighed the most of any of my children at birth but was also the sickest. He was in and out of the hospital for various reasons but was the easiest child to take care of. He was so happy all the time. For the next six months, I really don't know what happened. I went through all the motions as a mom because I had two other children at home and a husband to take care of. I called it "autopilot," doing what needed to be done but not remembering what I did.

Autopilot is a term in aviation that means the routine duties of maintaining an aircraft's heading altitude and airspeed are accomplished automatically without human activity. The good side of autopilot is that it relieves the pilot to process other tasks because the routine is being taken care of. The negative side is that it's easy to get out of the logic loop; the pilot isn't considering the right and wrong of each task. The pilot is no longer in the decision-making loop. Although it can be valuable for information processing, at some point all pilots have to transition off autopilot or they'll crash.

IDENTITY REDEFINED

Each of Nancy Miller's four stages—*surviving, searching, settling,* and *separating*—has circumstances that define conditional or temporary identities. God called Gideon a mighty warrior; Gideon replied that he was weak. Both identity definitions were valid from the respective points of view, but guess which one became the anchor for transformation?

If you say God's definition, you are mostly right, but don't discount Gideon's. His definition of himself, his sense of identity, was accurate in the moment. If you read the biblical account, you will see that God never rebuked Gideon for his conditional perspective. Instead, that temporary identity became the building block for what Gideon would become. To grow into the permanent place of one of history's great liberators, he had to "start in the winepress," right where he lived, weaknesses and all.

Gideon was at first overwhelmed, fearful, and couldn't believe what he was hearing from God. Why was he being given such an enormous, daunting commission? All he could cling to was that God was going to be with him. He was going to experience what it meant to live in God's empowerment, a newly defined identity above and beyond his own.

Clay can be shaped, or transformed, into a new identity with new purpose. Read the words of therapist Faith Raimer about clay.

Jars of Clay

> As mere mortals, we are like jars of clay—fragile yet durable. We are designed to hold contents that include a special combination of gifts from the Potter who made us and shapes us. These gifts, uniquely specific to each, are meant to be enjoyed and shared.
>
> For some of us, these gifts are obvious and easily mastered. But more often than not for most of us, they are not immediately recognized or imagined. Time and growth are prerequisites during maturation for a bud to come into full bloom. So it is with our gifts from the potter.
>
> Jars that have been damaged may not hold water like they used to—if that was what they were shaped for—but the way I see it, those cracks allow for light to shine from within. While scars remind us of what *was*, cracks can help to illuminate the beauty of what *is*.
>
> My history is part of who I am, but I am not my history.

IDENTITY REDEFINED IN SPITE OF CIRCUMSTANCES

In the search for peace in your redefined identity, the actions you decide to take—not only because of your circumstances, but also in spite of them—are significant. In spite of his feelings of weakness and his place in the winepress, Gideon reached up and climbed out of hiding from the problems, out of the winepress, and into the light where he could make a difference. Your actions of faith right now, even though you may not yet fully grasp your redefined identity, will become your ladder out of where you are and into the light.

The world promises fantastic results from positive thinking. Is it mental hype or denial? Is it a gift from God? And do you always have to know the difference? Obviously prolonged denial isn't a healthy perspective, but at the same time finding a positive outlook in any situation is a valuable first step. Dr. Caroline Leaf in her books *Who Switched Off My Brain* and *Switch On Your Brain: The Key to Peak Happiness, Thinking, and Health* extols the many chemical, physical, emotional, and spiritual rewards from the action of bringing your thoughts captive to faith, hope, and love. When you do so, you give your brain a chance for a respite of peace, altering your body's chemical response to the situation.

Truthfulness before God is never wrong. When you commune with God in private, you can best be straightforward about your frailty, any sense of being unprepared, or even a reality check that reveals a significant incompetency. His love remains consistent in spite of your words. When you are straightforward with God, you begin to move forward into His provisions, including prevailing peace. Courage too will surprise you. In the process you will encounter times when it's important to declare positively who God is ("God is my heavenly Father") and who you are ("I am becoming a great warrior").

Ephesians 2:10 says, "For we are God's handiwork, created in Christ Jesus to do good works, which God prepared in advance for us to do." When the Bible says the words *we are*, it's talking about *you*. When you personalize the verse by replacing the "we are" with "I am," you are allowing God to work His magnificent ability in your life. Internal realities form external realities sooner or later. So you can rightfully declare the truth of His words for your life, that you *are* God's workmanship and can do anything and everything necessary because He is empowering your persona and purpose.

The writer of Romans, in 8:37–39, inspires confidence in God's provision in terrible times. He writes, "No, in all these things we are more than conquerors through him who loved us. For I am convinced that neither death nor life, neither angels nor demons, neither the present nor the future, nor any powers, neither height nor depth, nor anything else in all creation, will be able to separate us from the love of God that is in Christ Jesus our Lord."

The deliberate choice to renew your mind, causing the negative nagging "I can't do this!" to morph into more positive inclinations, is an exercise in the right direction. You then come into agreement with God's vision as you act on this revelation from His heart. Doing so is not shoving the emotions down and putting on a pseudo brave face but making a genuine response to engage biblical truth. You emerge into someone you never dreamed you could be. And every small action you take, in spite of your circumstances, reveals God's nature to you and through you.

Your willingness to continue to petition God and lean on His understanding as greater than your own opens the way before you. It empowers you to step toward liberation from your conditional, temporary identities toward your God-given core identity, enveloped by His peace.

When the apostle Paul faced anxiety, he called out to the Lord for wisdom. The Lord's answer is recorded in 2 Corinthians 12:9. "He said to me, 'My grace is sufficient for you, for my power is made perfect in weakness.' Therefore, I will boast all the more gladly about my weaknesses, so that Christ's power may rest on me."

Who Me?

WHO ME?
YES YOU.
WHY ME?
I SAID.
WHAT FOR?
HE BORE.
HOW CAN?
I AM!

In Psalm 18:32 the psalmist declares, "It is God who arms me with strength and keeps my way secure."

Unless

A rose is a rose is a rose;
unless you know the God who created it.
A day is a day is a day;
unless you live it with the God who spoke it into existence.
A life is a life is a life;
unless you allow the Giver of Life to indwell it.

PRAY

Heavenly Father, in my weaknesses, pain, and suffering, I trust You to equip me with Your empowering presence. Grant me the strength I need. I trust by the power of the Holy Spirit that Your grace is sufficient for my needs today. I believe I am more than a conqueror because Your power is resting on me.

REFLECT

1. Are you feeling positive and energetic today or just plain wiped out? Can you identify with Gideon? Is God speaking to you through Gideon's story?

2. As a parent of a child dealing with special circumstances, you have identified yourself already in certain ways. You have the choice to take on or reject further identities that come from the comments and reactions of others to define or label you. You may have experienced expressions of respect, admiration, kindness, and love. Can you recall some of them? These are the warming, positive identities that only someone in your place is privileged to experience.

3. While you are still in the process of figuring out your new identity, there is a respite of peace waiting for you. Relax and take a deep breath as you read the Scriptures below. Smile at God's sparkling reflection of who you are.

    I am the salt of the earth (Matthew 5:13).
    I am the light of the world (Matthew 5:14).
    I am a child of God (John 1:12).
    I am a temple of God (1 Corinthians 3:16).
    God's spirit and His life dwell in me (1 Corinthians 6:19).
    I am a new creation (2 Corinthians 5:17).
    I am reconciled with God (2 Corinthians 5:18–19).
    I am God's handiwork (Ephesians 2:10).

4. Maybe you already have a network of parents who can openly share real-life stories, challenges, and victories. If not, you may want to consider starting one or joining one or becoming part of a parents chat group on the Internet. Choose whatever fits your lifestyle. (Joni and Friends is a good place to start online at http://www.joniandfriends.org.)

3

Transformation: Am I Melting?

Bewildered, stuck, and stretched
to transfiguring, redefined, and refined

AS YOUR FUNCTIONAL identity is being redefined, you are moving from spinning in place to regaining your forward momentum. Have you heard it said, "If you aren't moving forward, you're moving backward"? But why does it feel sometimes like you're on a hamster treadmill? Why does it feel like you are "melting away"?

WHAT IS TRANSFORMATION?

Transformation means to transform, to convert, or to change. It can also mean transfigure, reshape, rebuild, or pass through. Just the thought of transforming into a new state of being from the present may give you cause to want to shout out loud, "I need this and I need it now!" On the other hand, your thoughts may be more like, *"Are you kidding me? More change? What I really need now is a break!"*

A common metaphor for transformation is the lifespan of a butterfly. The early stage is known as the cocoon life, which has been described as caterpillar "melting." A caterpillar's body can be described as melting away almost completely before it begins to morph into a butterfly while it is in the chrysalis, or cocoon. A later stage, referred to as metamorphosis, is the time within the confines of the cocoon when the caterpillar transforms into its destiny as a butterfly. It is breathtaking to watch a worm-like, crawling creature change into an amazing winged beauty that can fly!

Marjorie shares about her transformation stages that at first she felt like she was stuck on the exercise wheel of a gerbil cage, running madly and getting nowhere fast. She couldn't find her way off the wheel or out of the cage.

Susan says her change of identity time was more like the early cocoon stage time, as if she were melting. Everything was changing. She had no idea what was happening or what was to come. She admitted that she and her husband were clueless as to what could come from resting in the process of taking on their latest commission as parents of a child with yet undefined but obvious special needs. What would this new creation, formed from the raw materials of each of their lives, look like? But they decided to watch and wait. What Susan found to her surprise was hope—a hope that soon enough there would be a revelation and a resurrection.

Jeremiah 29:11 says, "'For I know the plans I have for you,' declares the LORD, 'plans to prosper you and not to harm you, plans to give you hope and a future.'" Though Marjorie and Susan could not control what was happening or grasp its significance, God knew. He had a plan.

Gideon, God's mighty warrior, was also "cocooned" for a time. He would need God's help at each stage of his "becoming." Drastic changes were happening in him as he "melted" into who he was to become. Like Susan and Marjorie, he could not see in advance what he would look like and how he would interact with his world around him through his metamorphosis.

As you are cocooned and melt into your metamorphosis, try to remember that you have both temporary identities and a core identity. Your personal understanding of the functional identity you are struggling to live in right now is in a state of flux.

Consider some of the functional identity titles that might be added to your growing list. You may not have thought of yourself in these new ways before your transformation began. Among the myriad of other positive and poetic descriptions, consider yourself as becoming a treasure hunter, advocate, ambassador, athlete, pilot, inventor, geologist, educator, nurse, and Web specialist for research on parenting a child with special needs. No doubt you can think of even more.

HATS AND MORE HATS

As you assume the various roles of your present functional identity, you might think of them as putting on different hats. A word of caution here: Beware! Within that collection of hats could lie hidden a false identity that could trip you up! The false identity hat exists because of an irrational belief that if you just keep trying harder the way you are, you can achieve near perfection.

Perfection assumes that you have within yourself the strength to strive toward perfect behavior. It tells you that by your own efforts, you can get it all right and get control over your changing environment while doing it.

Is this trap of thinking familiar? Consider the many heroes who have had to face and overcome daunting obstacles, including Helen Keller, who became deaf and blind before age two, and modern day physicist and cosmologist Stephen Hawking, who suffers with ALS. History boasts of their accomplishments. Do their stories lead you to believe, "If they could do it, I should (must) be able to do it too?" That's not even a reasonable thought. Your "hat size" is different from theirs.

If you've sacrificed and pushed hard again and again, most likely you have found yourself falling short in your heroic attempts at becoming the perfect parent. Nearly everyone recognizes at some point that something is intrinsically shaky in his or her identity when there is the false notion of perfection through personal strength alone. Sometimes parents expect of themselves what God Himself would never expect of them.

Whenever you are tempted to put on every "hat" out there, signifying your varied roles and then expect to fulfill them all perfectly, consider saying this line to yourself: "I'm wearing enough hats, thank you. Talk to the hand!" (Translation: "I'm not accepting the idea that I have to be perfect in every transitional stage as the only alternative to describing success or failure as a parent.")

Yes, you can do more than you originally thought you could, but expecting perfection can assail your sense of gratitude for what has changed already for the good. Yes, God is with you. He alone can empower the difference you long to experience. Yes, you are becoming a quality, educated, Spirit-filled, capable parent. That metamorphosis includes being able to say, "No (or not now)." And yes, an occasional wise "stepping away" does not change the positive truths about who you are, what you have accomplished, and what is yet to be accomplished.

You've probably had to do some stretching and may have some fairly large "stretch marks" to show for it. They are a sign of birthing too, a sign that your life is taking on a new form. Your core and functional identity are in recovery. You are melting in God's cocoon. You are being redefined, reshaped, and empowered. As transformation happens, lean on your heavenly Father, His Son Jesus, and the guiding Holy Spirit. You reach. God responds. You are a partaker in His life-giving grace and peace.

2 Corinthians 12:9 says, "But he said to me, 'My grace is sufficient for you, for my power is made perfect in weakness.' Therefore I will boast all the more gladly about my weaknesses, so that Christ's power may rest on me."

REDEFINED AND REFINED

God is revealing your dynamic persona and purpose. All the while, your core persona is anchored in His family, as His child. While you are being redefined, you are being continually refined, energized, made vibrant, and yes, even vigorous. Your values are evolving. You are gaining a deeper understanding of His evaluation of a life. With God's transforming power, you are able to fulfill your parental responsibilities with a renewed sense of honor. Psalm 71:21 says, "You will increase my honor and comfort me once more" (Psalm 84:11; 112:9).

Fingers of Truth

Fingers of truth readied upon the violin
bring forth their sound
as the bow of understanding
moves across its path.

A Better End

Understanding, a warm welcome friend,
lends to the friendship of knowledge and wisdom
a better end.

IDENTITY ANCHOR

Joan's anchoring phrase was, "Get a grip girl, and don't drift." Carl would often chant, "Man up!" Tom challenged himself by saying, "Snap out of it, or walk like a man." No matter what anchoring phrase you use to keep your identity steady, most of them fall short when the pressure of responsibility increases drastically. Consuming demands on your time and energy are likely to feel as though you have an anchor dragging along behind you in a strong current that controls you.

The only anchoring truth that is strong enough to hold you in place is the one weighted by the realization of the depth of God's love. When you turned your life over to God, you opened your heart to His Son Jesus as your Lord, Savior, personal friend, and brother. As you welcomed in the Holy Spirit, you became part of another family—God's personal family. He is your heavenly Father! You are His child, perfect in His sight. Here, then, is a better anchor: quote and requote a Scripture verse such as Philippians 4:12–13 (NKJV), "I know how to be abased, and I know how to abound. Everywhere and in all things I have learned both to be full and to be hungry, both to abound and to suffer need. I can do all things through Christ who strengthens me."

Jason's continual declaration is, "His goodness is everlasting." This reminder supersedes the daily negative input he faces with the challenges he and his wife encounter as parents. They both agree that "the God life" is about progressively getting better acquainted with what it means to know God and love one another as His children.

A life-altering identity transformation is happening for you right now. Its new family status, new family authority, new family members, and new family dynamics are all yours too. You have access through Jesus to the Creator of the Universe as your personal Father God (Ephesians 2:18). You are in training. You are becoming Christ-like. The Holy Spirit is your comfort and guide for help in every situation you face.

Your identity transformation is a grand paradigm shift. It alters your perspective of hope for this life and for the eternity that awaits you and your family. Like no other, God's words of truth can become the well-weighted anchor to your identity. There is no other like Him.

EXTRAVAGANT INVITATION

An extravagant invitation is being extended to you. Consider how Julie responds to the invitation in her story.

The Extravagant Invitation

"You are invited into a divine, royal adventure."

When Julie heard that incredulous sentence in a parents group meeting, she responded, "How so? What makes what I am going through an invitation by and into divinity? That seems so off base from where I am and what I need to know right now." And then she listened.

"At first, it was like a little tickle inside, hard to describe. It started small. My head still didn't understand and my thoughts felt like it was a waste of time to sit there, but I couldn't deny that growing, lovely sense inside while I listened to the group leader speak."

The leader went on to say to her, "The royal adventure is so extravagant and a gift to the soul."

"What's so extravagant, and how can that be true?"

"It's not an invitation to human excellence."

Julie retorted, "I should hope not. Who wouldn't give up if that were the requirement?"

"It's not you but His Holy Spirit, His Grace, His Glory, His personal presence as His child and heir to eternal life. Julie, you have an inexpressible potential. You are invited to engage, take up, and experience the mystery of His ways expressed in your core identity. This identity changes how you value your required activities and life in general. It soaks you in truth that overrules the daily grind that is challenging you into believing that you are so much less than."

"Less than what?" she asked.

"Less than whatever it is you feel you need to be in this moment."

The thought of having an identity that was defined within God's divine nature alone was so far from Julie's thought life at the time. "I was more interested in controlling my emotions and tips that would help me find time and space for the workload to lighten," she remembers.

"It's more than an entry point of a cleansed past, or even a strengthening for the now. It reaches into the realms of the Kingdom of God for its provision and personal presence."

"Where is this leading?" Julie asked.

"It takes you into the valuable treasures of God's extravagant mercies, to the feasting in the fullness of His enabling grace. It's His ability in your life. Your role as a parent of a child with special needs is an adventure. Your identity as a child of God, a child of the King Jesus, and a resting place for the Holy Spirit in your spirit, is an unlimited adventure. It carries within it potential for a royal journey in every undertaking. It's now, and it's future."

Julie left the meeting feeling exhilarated. She had that feeling of wanting to stretch her arms out and take off running. And yet she was still pondering what it all could mean.

Later she would know. "It made a difference. My perspective began to change. I learned that no matter what strategy I applied to keep a healthy identity steady, most of them fell short as the reoccurring, consuming demands of time and energy began to create a strong current, dragging my anchor with them. There was only one truth that kept me stable. It was that I was learning my core identity and purpose was in Christ Jesus my Lord, my brother, and He had become my friend. This and this alone was my anchor."

Over time Julie's sense of wellness grew stronger in this new identity as a child of the King, her personal Lord and Savior. She couldn't wrap her understanding around all the beautiful sounding words that were shared that day, but she knew it had been a significant meeting. It was going to make a huge difference. As years passed, she realized it was the birthing place where her core identity was anchored and where her core values began reforming.

The Holy Spirit is with you today to inspire your thinking, reinvent your sense of capability, and cocoon you into the melting place where new life is formed. You have become and are still becoming a new creation. Jesus said it best. "Therefore, if anyone is in Christ, the new creation has come. The old has gone, the new is here" (2 Corinthians 5:17).

It's not just a little improvement; it's a metamorphosis. It's not working harder or getting a little more ability than you used to have. It's a complete redefining of who you are in Christ. It's real, and it's expanding.

Scripture declares, "Jesus Christ is the same yesterday and today and forever" (Hebrews 13:8). You are transitioning, transforming, transfiguring, into His character. When you surrendered your heart to the eternal and unchanging Lord Jesus, inviting all that He is into your life, you received His indwelling presence.

You are on a healthy, life-giving journey. You realize it's good to pace yourself because it is not a short sprint but a long-distance run. The Holy Spirit is available to you all along the way. In truth, He's right there with you, not just when you think you need Him but all the time. His still, small voice amid the noise of thunder and the winds will guide you.

WHO OUT THERE IS PERFECT?

Your prior expectation of having to be a perfect parent *all the time in every role* is losing its power. After all, there can be only one perfect Father and one perfect child: the heavenly Father and His Son Jesus Christ. Humankind is formed in His likeness and image but without the capacity for perfection, as you would probably define perfection. When the Bible in Matthew 5:48 reads, "Be perfect, therefore, as your heavenly Father is perfect," it's talking about being complete.

Colossians 2:2–3 states the apostle Paul's idea of completion. "My goal is that they may be encouraged in heart and united in love, so that they may have the full riches of complete understanding, in order that they may know the mystery of God, namely Christ, in whom are hidden all the treasures of wisdom and knowledge." As the ending of 1 John 4:12 explains, it is God's love in Christ that is being "made complete in us."

If you redefine the word *perfect* as maturing toward a state of perfection, you can identify with it as a description of yourself right now. You, perfect? Smile and have an inward grin. No, you don't do everything perfectly, and you have not yet arrived at the perfection that will be experienced only in the heavenly realm one day. For today, for now, however, perfection is forming in you.

Consider an apple tree or a tomato plant. When you see those little round balls of not yet fully mature fruit growing on them, you are excited. They are perfect even if they are not as far along as they will be later. Green now, yes. But soon red and delicious produce will appear. They, small and green, are maturing. They are perfect just as they are right now.

Humankind has a forever timeline. You weren't just born for today or this life on earth. You were born to live forever. You have an eternal existence as His child. Your perfect Father God has promised a perfect family and a perfect home in a perfect environment: one day you and your children will live with your heavenly Father in that perfect place. You will be together in His big, gloriously happy family. Nothing you do before or after then will be wasted because all in His family continue to fulfill their personal destinies throughout eternity. In the meantime, there are lovely discoveries of beautiful life experiences, maturing your fruit as a loving capable parent or caregiver.

CONNECTEDNESS AND HARMONY

Everyone has a need to feel connected: connected to faith, connected to hope, and connected to love. When you sense connected harmonies in your life, it is natural to have a secure but not complete feeling of connectedness. The eternal connection, however, is to God and His Son and our Savior, Jesus Christ. It is the most critical connection that needs to be established, the ultimate in feeling completely connected.

For Christians who choose the eternal connection, it is very important to remember that your citizenship is in heaven. Scripture declares that you are no more aliens and strangers from the promises of God, but in Christ you are heaven-born citizens (Ephesians 2:19; 1 Peter 1:4–5). No wonder nothing here will ever completely satisfy. Nothing here may ever seem perfectly fit or perfectly balanced. Nothing here may ever completely meet that inner yearning for beauty, contentment, peace, harmony, and balance except a personal relationship with the Lord Jesus Christ. Only He can give that "Aha" restful, satisfied sense in the soul everyone is desperate to experience.

In response to your choice, the gift of the Holy Spirit within you brings the potential for supernatural peace and His miraculous, harmonious relationship with God that are eternal. Isaiah 32:17–18 says, "The fruit of that righteousness will be peace; its effect will be quietness and confidence forever. My people will live in peaceful dwelling places, in secure homes, in undisturbed places of rest."

The Holy Spirit pours the love of God into your heart, giving you the ability to face each day with a stable awareness of well-being and satisfaction. As you grow in your walk with God, you will find that He is training you in continuous harmony. He is teaching you how to maintain its delicate balance during the perilous times.

Read the words of therapist Faith Raimer on harmony.

Harmony

Most of us enjoy the peace we derive from harmony. And some of us fight harder than others to maintain it. In fact, we often go to great measures to avoid conflict or discord. It is an option that may or may not be the best solution.

For an individual, harmony equates to calm, inner balance and tranquility. One way to achieve harmony is by choosing to be lovingly authentic with our "offenders" while purposing to seek resolution. It may not always be accomplished, but it is always worth the attempt. We are expected to do all we can do and at the same time allow God to do His part. I once heard someone say, "The effort belongs to me, and the results belong to God."

Harmony can also be achieved when combining or arranging those things that are not the same. Examples: We want to live in harmony with our neighbors; we would like all family members to agree on which restaurant to go to; and furniture style and wall color selection can help set the tone and flow in our homes. Musically speaking, harmony results from playing different notes and/or instruments together to create a pleasing sound. It is a treat to watch an orchestra bring sound to life before our eyes, particularly though not solely with pieces that are familiar to us.

King Solomon stated, "There is nothing new under the sun" (Eccl. 1:9). With all due respect for his wisdom, he probably never heard the nearly blind jazz virtuoso Art Tatum on piano; composer, bandleader and virtuoso Charles Mingus on bass; Miles Davis or Dizzy Gillespie on trumpet; or the uniquely personal vocal style of Billie Holiday. Of

> course, Solomon's point was that many things seem new because the past is so easily and quickly forgotten. As one who loved beauty and art, he would no doubt be captivated by the awe-inspiring harmony of jazz musicians as together and in turn they create their sound.
>
> Yes, music and song continue to be written, recorded, and played for our listening pleasure. What's more, we have been invited by the Master himself ("He put a new song in my mouth, a hymn of praise" Ps. 40:3) to live in harmony as we "sing to the Lord a new song, for he has done marvelous things" (Ps. 98:1).
>
> Can you picture what it must be like in heaven? Just imagine the voices of "thousands upon thousands" of angels encircling the throne and singing together in praise to the Lamb of God (Rev. 5:11, 12). We can be assured this is just a hint of the harmony that will be ours to enjoy for all eternity. The day will come when we are invited to join with that mighty and melodious chorus, but for now let us continue to bring heavenly harmony into our world as we are inspired and able. May we have ears to hear God's gift of music and be willing to sing along in heavenly harmony now.

With your choice of eternal connectedness and access to His harmony comes the expectation of better times ahead, or at least better handled times. Each time ahead, as it unfolds, will require another choice, a choice to believe God and trust Him no matter what you feel and see in the natural. Hebrews 11:1 says, "Now faith is confidence in what we hope for and assurance about what we do not see."

It sounds incredulous when we read apostle Paul's exclamation in 2 Corinthians 12:10, "That is why, for Christ's sake, I delight in weaknesses, in insults, in hardships, in persecutions, in difficulties. For when I am weak, then I am strong." Like him, your choice is a choice of faith. Romans 5:1–5 can be read this way (paraphrased, with personal application added), "Therefore, having been justified by faith, you have peace with God through your Lord Jesus Christ, through whom also you have access by faith into this grace in which you stand, and rejoice in hope of the glory of God. And not only that, but you also glory in tribulations, knowing that tribulation produces perseverance; and perseverance, character; and character, hope. Now hope does not disappoint because the love of God has been poured out in your heart by the Holy Spirit who was given to you."

Many times you may not see or feel contentment, but at the same time you are asking Him for it; it's wisdom to be saying inside, "I choose contentment, harmony, and peace." It's the choice of faith in the face of contrary circumstances, and it brings with it great gain from God. Paul declares in 1 Timothy 6:6, "Godliness with contentment is great gain."

As you make each choice to believe God and trust Him in spite of your feelings or outward evidence, it is much like practicing a musical instrument. The coordination and harmonious sounds of learning to play an instrument don't come easily at first, but they do come in time. You are growing. You are changing, transforming, and being transfigured. Your capacity is expanding into the fullness of a divinely inspired persona and purpose.

Ever Still

Grown, I am still growing...
Known, I am ever knowing...
Filled, yet always filling...
To the fullness of the measure
and the stature of Christ...
I am transforming.

PRAY

Father God, lift me from the sense of driven duty today. Grant me insight and revelation into more of what it means to be Your beloved child. Thank you for the invitation into an identity that values what You value and lets go of what is not necessary. When I feel like I'm going nowhere, help me be aware of Your cocooning workmanship. I trust You are transforming me. More is going on than I can see or feel. I am in process. Grace and peace are working a beautiful transformation in my life. I gratefully give You praise for Your royal invitation into a royal adventure.

REFLECT

There is a continual, forming work of the Holy Spirit in you for the purpose of not only taking you to heaven one day but also daily forming you into the likeness of His Son and your personal Lord Jesus.

1. Identify an area you are aware the Holy Spirit is maturing you. As you consider your progress, what positive reactions can you see in contrast to what you used to experience?

2. Pick one aspect of parenting that remains a major challenge. Take a minute to tell your heavenly Father you trust His forming work of the Spirit in you and give Him this area. You might even write it on a piece of paper, lift it to Him, and then throw it in the trash as a symbol of trusting His love to continue bringing you into wiser and more Spirit-led actions.

3. All praise goes, as Jude says, "To him who is able to keep you from stumbling and to present you before his glorious presence without fault and with great joy" (Jude v. 24). What comes to your mind when you read these words?

4

The Zones: What Now?

Drained, dreading, lost, searching to healthier, hopeful, provisioned, and empowered

YOU ARE GAINING healthy perspective. You are moving from spinning emotions such as frustration, hopelessness, and restlessness into the more positive zones, where you can find glorious respites of patience, a graceful peace, and a hopeful outlook. Trust is peeking over the horizon.

All parents need help from time to time in finding new ways to provide the peaceful, hope-filled home families long to call their own. Children are especially sensitive to the atmosphere in their home environment. The heavenly Father's supernatural provision can help you maintain a healthy home atmosphere with a prevailing sense of security and peace.

PROVISION

Carmella's story underscores the truth of the heavenly Father's provision.

Gentleness, Save Me!

After a while, I settled into a more predictable pattern of family life. Then slam! Financial constraints required me to find a job, any job that helped meet the needs. The children were in elementary school, and my husband was up and out of the home early, so it fell to me to get the kids ready, pack the lunches, and get myself out the door and to work on time. Regularly, my third grade child with ADHD would lose her shoes, misplace her books, or present me with some annoying detail. The weight of it all began to irritate me incessantly.

One morning as I was running down the stairs to get the kids in the car, once again she just stood there, not ready. I was going to be late again! I could feel my frustration fever rising. Again I was going to be reprimanded by my boss. Why me? Why couldn't this child ever just do as she was asked?

This emotional reaction spiraled from irritability to bitterness and resentment. I was in deep need of an attitude adjustment. Deep sigh, again. The search for answers was desperate. This time it was for me. I thought I had a handle on these emotional upheavals, and now, this raw reaction.

The eye of a storm is the place where the raging winds come to a halt and everything is calm. Clear skies, a peaceful place—at least for a short time. But who wants to live in the unpredictable, ever moving eye of a hurricane? I longed for more than just a softer tone and a little more patience. When was peace going to prevail?

Gentleness. That's it. That's what I want. I have to find a way for peace to show up in gentleness.

I began researching Scripture on the value and power of gentleness. I cherished my children and I wanted them to know it. Was it possible I could project this godly virtue to calm the atmosphere of our home? I didn't want to remain the short-tempered, angry mother I had recently become. In my search, I discovered these verses.

Philippians 4:5, "Let your gentleness be evident to all. The Lord is near."

1 Timothy 6:11, "But you, man of God, flee from all this, and pursue righteousness, godliness, faith, love, endurance and gentleness."

At first I wondered if reading and praying, claiming these words as my own personal inheritance in Christ Jesus my Lord, was making a difference. Key words: At first. Then came the miracle day. There she stood again, disheveled. She had no lunch, no shoes, and one sock in hand. And I had no time! As I started downstairs, my emotions boiling and ready to flare, what came out of my mouth shocked me. Instead of yelling at my daughter, I heard myself holler at the top of my lungs, "Gentleness, save me!" Pause, shock, silence, eye of the storm moment—OMG! He did it!

The gentle One, my loving heavenly Father, through the supernatural provision of the Holy Spirit, had resourced me in that crucial moment with a generous dose of His grace. There I stood, halfway down the stairs, stunned for a few seconds at what I had just heard myself shout. Instead of anger it was a declaration of faith and desperate plea at the same time. "Gentleness, save me!"

Slowly a tiny smile crept across my face. His glorious provision had just rescued my soul and my children's morning. What started as a brief respite in the eye of my storm was just the beginning of a transformation in me. God was showing me calm and trust as I began to lean into Him more each day. I was learning and delighted to discover the Holy Spirit was helping me be the parent I longed to be. I was settling in and becoming new at the same time. I was growing in His grace!

"Not that I have already obtained all this, or have already been made perfect, but I press on to take hold of that for which Christ Jesus took hold of me. Brothers, I do not consider myself yet to have taken hold of it. But one thing I do: Forgetting what is behind and straining toward what is ahead, I press on toward the goal to win the prize for which God has called me heavenward in Christ Jesus" (Philippians 3:12–14).

WHAT'S NEXT?

After a respite in the eye of the storm comes the second force. It's often even worse than the first part of the storm. But having experienced God's provision of peace, you are armed by His grace and ready to face whatever comes next (John 16:33).

Have you noticed how little if any understanding comes from pursuing the "why me" question? That question, if you even want to call it one instead of a debilitating complaint, is seldom satisfied. Even when an answer is obvious, it rarely helps any of the parental process to dwell on it. The good news is that the "why me" begins to meld into the "what now is more practical and healthier" question. It becomes a stepping-stone to the creation of an internal peace zone.

SEARCHING

The *searching* stage for parents of children with special needs overlaps the initial *surviving* stage. It continues to be a component of the stages that follow, as you will see in the chapters that follow. Searching is the first step in regaining some sense of control. It begins with questions that are both inner and outer directed.

Inner searching asks, "Why? Who's at fault?" It seeks to place blame. These questions can be harsh and judgmental. In an attempt to make sense of your circumstances, you may target genetics, or what you did or didn't do. It's common to blame yourself.

Outer searching is usually more productive, more positive. It asks, "What's wrong, and how can it be fixed?" It looks for diagnosis and treatment. Parents who once described themselves as easygoing or passive can develop an unexpected assertiveness during their search for answers.

Elaine's story typifies the searching stage, where searching yields some answers and some surprises.

Searching for Answers

It is very difficult to find out information on a disease when the doctors are in the dark about it. At the time the doctors diagnosed my son, Matt, the medical field really didn't know what caused Duchenne's, which is only one form of muscular dystrophy. Since then they've identified about forty different types, all neuromuscular diseases that affect individuals differently.

> Back in the early 1980s when I was searching, we didn't have computers like we do today. We relied almost exclusively on the medical profession for all of our information on disease. So we took what we had, whatever information and help we could gather, and went with it.
>
> My family and friends were great during this time of transition. They helped me put together major fundraisers for MDA in our area to raise funds and awareness, including Roll and Stroll, Bike for Life, and a bowling event. I would take Matt with me to preschools so the children could talk to him about not walking. Matt did walk until he was about seven or eight years old, and then he went into a wheelchair. So I had many opportunities to share my story, as did Matt. One friend I met along the way had two sons with Duchenne's and was a single mother, doing it all alone along with the help of her parents.
>
> Everywhere I went, I picked the brain of anyone who would listen to me, including all the doctors at the clinics. Along the way, I found little help but much encouragement.

In his time of searching, Gideon, the mighty warrior and biblical hero, continually questioned God and asked for reassurance. Judges 6:17 records these words of his: "If now I have found favor in your eyes, give me a sign that it is really you talking to me." And get this! He goes on to ask God to wait while he goes and gets an offering to give to Him. And God waits! Verse 18b records God's response: "And the LORD said, 'I will wait until you return.'" In verse 23, God reassures Gideon again. "But the LORD said to him, 'Peace! Do not be afraid. You are not going to die.'"

Have you experienced this kind of white knuckle, heart-pounding, raw emotion while probing for answers and wading through myriads of research information? The key is to keep pressing in until you have a personal revelation of the God of peace. Keep doing what you know to do until you sense God's heart in your heart, His confidence in your soul, and His assignment compelling you forward. There, in that place of revelation, creativity will flourish.

PEACE ZONE DIVERS

Peace has physical and emotional effects, as does the absence of peace. When you enter into a peaceful setting, it is almost tangible. It's like stepping on a cushioned welcome mat. When it's gone, it feels like someone yanked the mat out from under your feet! All those godly, loving attributes you wish to engender such as gentleness, goodness, kindness, self-control, and perseverance can feel out of reach, like sunken treasures. And where was it you stored that diving gear?

Peace is also powerful! The Bible forecasts that the God of Peace will crush Satan under the feet of believers (Romans 16:20). The Bible challenges believers to seek and find peace, a needed provision, especially during inner searching. "Let the peace of Christ rule in your hearts, since as members of one body you were called to peace. And be thankful" (Colossians 3:15).

Peace is so much more than just a calm, emotional response to your latest upset. It's an inward grace ability (Galatians 5) and more. Grace is often described as undeserved mercy. But more than receiving something that cannot be earned, grace is God's empowering presence, enabling you to become what He has uniquely designed in you and to empower you to accomplish your God-given purpose. As you live from the inner resource of His personal presence, you discover it becomes easier and easier to access the characteristics of His grace ability. You can actually begin to thrive in grace. 1 Peter 1:2b says, "Grace and peace be yours in abundance."

Elaine's story about her son, Matt, who suffered with Duchenne's muscular dystrophy, moves from one of searching for answers to finding peace.

"It was obvious that our son, Matt, was going to go to heaven years before we had hoped and prayed," said Elaine. "I realized I had to plan for the future without him even though my life at the present was saturated in caring for him. Who would I be? How would I find peace in the absence of my son?"

Elaine began writing letters to herself, preparing for her son's death, that she would read monthly or when she was at a particularly emotional time. She interviewed other parents about their feelings after their children entered heaven. And she wrote letters to herself about them to read after her son's death to help her press on. She also got involved in other children's lives before her son died. Over time those children became like her grandchildren. They brought her the pleasure and joy of an adult-child relationship that helped fill the void after her son was no longer living.

Mark's searching led him to peace as well. His words about his journey prove that the words in the Bible have inborn ability to transform and transfigure our whole response to life.

> In the beginning, the biblical truths may not integrate your spirit and soul and have defining effects on your body. They may feel like they are separate, and although you believe them, it's hard to understand how they will make a significant difference. Maybe they feel like they are just religion and this is real life on the ground, and you have to focus on what's happening here and now, not some day when. The why of it all may not be clear for quite a while, if ever. The internal transformation spoken about in the Bible may seem impossible.
>
> God's Word is not just for the times when problems arise and there is a need for more understanding, strength, or peace. As I dived into the Bible, I was becoming. I was growing in my likeness to Christ in His life, death, burial, and resurrection. It was making a difference in me as I read how Jesus integrated the truth of how He handled disappointment, pain, and suffering because God was with Him. It was a deepening revelation. It became a well of salvation. One of the emerging surprises was joy.
>
> His encouragement to others was that it is possible, it can happen. There is a resource over and above our own. The Holy Spirit is here to comfort, guide, and hold our whole being together when life wants to hit it with a hammer and shatter it into tiny little pieces.

Peace is a safety zone. The New Testament tells several stories in which parents brought their children to Jesus. In each one, He lovingly placed His hands on the children and prayed for them. His manner had to be gentle and kind, communicating safety and peace, for children to want to crowd around Him. He welcomed them into His close, personal space—His zone of peace.

COURAGE ZONE

When you become willing to give up the security of the known, new opportunity can be created, and growth can occur. Isn't that what you signed up for when you became a parent in the first place? Parenting, when fully embraced, is a call to the risk takers, brave heart seekers, quality heart givers, and particularly to parents of children with special needs. Parenting isn't for cowards, but it can translate cowards into courageous, mighty men and women of God!

In Christ you find not only peace but another zone, a "courage zone." It is an inner place where your mind and heart can abide in Him that supersedes the outer, raw experiences of parenting. It's also an outer place built on experience. As you parent a child with special needs, you begin to expand the perimeter of your courage zone. You accept greater challenges, and your personal and parenting confidence increase. It's a paradox. You become more and more at ease when you courageously take on the discomfort inherent in the required risk-taking.

As you think about your expanding courage zone, read 1 Chronicles 4:10. "Jabez cried out to the God of Israel, 'Oh, that you would bless me and enlarge my territory! Let your hand be with me, and keep me from harm so that I will be free from pain.' And God granted his request." His territory expanded, and yours is too.

Meredith panicked the first time her son Isaac fell forward on the hard tile, his tooth cutting through his lip. She looked at the bleeding. Fearful and desperately seeking advice, she called her mom and dad. "Can you watch the other boys while I go to the hospital? Isaac has had an accident." A week later, Isaac's baby brother Jacob, walking wobbly, tripped over a toy and fell on the same hard tile. He cut his lip as well. That time, no one got a call. Meredith's courage zone had expanded, and she handled the situation on her own.

"It's simple," Meredith said, "Not easy, but simple. You just get better at knowing what to do the more you practice doing it. It's more than just getting numb to repeated situations. Things don't ruffle you the same way they used to. Instead you have an inward, peaceful courage that carries over into the upcoming unknown as well."

Athletes understand what they call being "in the zone." It's a universal phenomenon experienced by almost all the great ones. So what is this zone? And how does it affect athletic performance? How do athletes find it? Not surprisingly, sport psychologists have been asking these questions for many years. Luckily, they have come up with a few interesting and helpful conclusions

In the simplest terms, *zone* (or *flow*, as some sport psychologists call it), is generally described as where athletes can perform their highest achievements. It's where they can reach their stunning best and spectacular compared to their peers. Their best may be a world record or just a great shot. Sports enthusiasts, active or arm chair, can recount endlessly with wide-eyed excitement the details of an athlete caught on camera while in the zone. "Did you see that guy? Did you see how cool he looked? It was like he was totally relaxed, as if he was just taking a bite of his favorite sandwich as he just slammed it in place!"

The zone for athletes is a place of super performance where even the best can reach a level that is beyond their usual abilities. When they get into the zone, they feel unstoppable and often are. It's a mindset.

Acts 17:28 says, "In him we live and move and have our being," and the apostle Paul says, "Those who live in accordance with the Spirit have their minds set on what the Spirit desires" (Romans 8:5b). What do these verses and the zone have to do with parenting? One of the key characteristics of athletes in the zone is said to be their ability to ignore negative thoughts. They have a higher self-esteem and confidence, and their performance shows it.

For Christians, living in the Spirit, inner abiding with Christ, is similar to what athletes call being in the zone. In His provision of grace, you can accomplish things far beyond your own abilities. You can, like the famed athletes, become unstoppable. There peace prevails, and there performance is enhanced by the Holy Spirit, who also brings a confident expectation of good to come—more than you could hope for on your own.

You're not guaranteed to land in "the zone" all of the time, but in getting ready, you're making yourself available to grow, building strength upon strength. Like the apostle Paul, you can say, "I press on toward the goal to win the prize for which God has called me heavenward in Christ Jesus" (Philippians 3:14).

For you as a parent, reaching the zone is not about striving to achieve something you don't have. It's more about discovering what you have been given, freely given by God. You are becoming something you never realized you could be or do. This becoming is born out of your spiritual DNA—your God-given identity and purpose. It's His gift. "Therefore we do not lose heart. Though outwardly we are wasting away, yet inwardly we are being renewed day by day" (2 Corinthians 4:16). "Whew," you can say, "I'm not going to have to work this up on my own!"

Remember, Gideon didn't feel like a mighty warrior when the angel came to him with the new job description. No one would have guessed he would be chosen to lead his people. He didn't look like someone who could help his family, his country, or serve God. Nevertheless, while he was still weak and things looked hopeless, God called him a mighty warrior. The same powerful words God gave to Gideon can be your own now.

Describe yourself out loud. Use these or other words of your choosing. "I am a peaceful and courageous warrior living in the Spirit of Grace Himself. I have the Author of Peace living inside me. I can do all things through Christ Jesus, who is right now strengthening me!"

You are in process of discovering your true persona and purpose, not just what you can do on your own strength under pressure. As you continue searching and reaching beyond where you are, you'll be surprised how you experience what God had in mind all along. Do you remember the movie *Back to the Future?* You are going back to your original spiritual DNA, and then you are coming into the present and future with the realization of who you really are. It's profoundly transfiguring your future.

Read these words from therapist Faith Raimer in which she explains courage in the face of obstacles.

In the Face of Obstacles

> American gymnast Paul Hamm was in first place after three out of six rotations in the Men's (all-around) Olympic Gymnastics (Athens 2004). He was practically guaranteed the gold medal with his next event, a vault,

because he had never missed a landing in any prior competition. That expectation was quickly shattered when during his landing, he stumbled and crashed into the judges' table.

Shocked and humiliated, Hamm watched as his standing plummeted from 1st to 12th place. His reality suffered a crushing blow along with the hopes for success of his Olympic teammates and the USA. Feeling the weight of the world on his shoulders for Hamm was not just a figure of speech. In a later interview, he admitted knowing he had only to take one small step to keep from falling and possibly gain a slightly higher ranking, but he was not willing to settle for anything less than perfect.

Like Hamm, you might not have considered something like a stumble. Or, like others, you might have wanted to throw in the towel and quit or wondered if all the years and cheers to get there were going to end like this?

Instead of quitting, Hamm used his God-given ability to think about his options for the next event. He reasoned that a strong finish might still award him third place overall and a bronze medal. He determined to make a swift shift in his mindset and go for it. He would have to fight like never before to accomplish it.

What happened next was stunning. Hamm went from 12th to 4th to 1st place, with a resulting score (57.823) that was twelve-thousandths of a point ahead of his closest competitor, South Korea's Kim Dae Eun (57.811). The crowd roared with approval at the miracle they had just witnessed. Hamm not only won by the closest finish ever in Olympic Men's Gymnastics, but his was one of the greatest comebacks in Olympic history.

There are times when we feel far from heroic and times when helplessness can actually be to our advantage. In Hamm's case with "nothing left to lose," his door of opportunity opened to a new possibility. It wasn't what he had dreamed of, but with effort he could turn it to gain.

I have found it isn't the failed attempt or limitation that blocks the way to personal attainment as much as it is the time we spend licking our wounds. Like Hamm, we need to get up from where we fell, brush ourselves off, and get back on track.

My older sister and I both used a self-coaching call: "Shape up, Raimer!" for a mindset shift to change. Sound silly? It works. Taking time to honor your feelings and emote is a good thing. So is a personal reminder to stop, and it works better if the coaching voice is your own. In that way, you are giving yourself permission to act in a way more empowered in the doing.

Hamm may not be typical, but he is an example of humans being human. And like him, we can use our God-given ability to direct our mind to focus on a concentrated effort in order to achieve a goal in the face of obstacles.

Still, there are those times when nothing seems to help. Our Lord knows when we hit those times. In fact, He has provided us with a cornucopia of sweet Scriptures meant to give us hope and soothe our souls. One of the many soul-soothing, healing balms we can apply is found in Isaiah 41:10. "So do not fear, for I am with you; do not be dismayed, for I am your God. I will strengthen you and help you; I will uphold you with my righteous right hand."

He wants you to know He loves you and is prepared to meet you right where you are. Are you willing to meet Him there? The effort is up to you. The results are up to God. Are you ready to go for it? You can begin by taking just one small step: TODAY I GIVE MYSELF PERMISSION TO ________________________.

GETTING IN THE ZONE

Athletes get themselves ready to perform in the zone in three ways: practice, devotion, and immersion. Each builds on the other. Achieving flow, being in the zone, gives them a remarkable advantage. To you, flow or zone might just sound like nothing but more hard work. Your active trust in the resources God has placed within you is where you are gaining significant enlargement. You are becoming an athlete in the zone as well as a treasure hunter, always ready to discover the beauty of His graces and the creativity and wonder of His ways, energizing your parenting.

Philippians 4:13 says, "I have strength for all things in Christ Who empowers me [I am ready for anything and equal to anything through Him Who infuses inner strength into me; I am self-sufficient in Christ's sufficiency]" (AMP).

Flow in the Spirit of God gives you a remarkable advantage. As you continue to refuse unhealthy imaginations, you bring your thoughts captive to the truth in Christ Jesus. You become a transformed overcomer. You are a wise player in the field of parenting. Peace not only visits you in the eye of the hurricane, but it also takes up residence in your life and home (2 Corinthians 10:5). Boldness, courage, and wisdom sprint with you in each new challenge.

Although many articles describe the zone, researchers are uncertain about what enables athletes to get into that place of super performance and stay there. But, interestingly enough, they are able to determine what brings them out of it—either fear or anger. These are also the two main attacks that the enemy to our soul sends to keep us from living in the Spirit. His wily plan is to jolt us out of the God-given, God-empowered zone.

You are a devoted parent. It is possible to excel in the skill like a champion athlete. You make the choice. You practice the skill. The rest is up to the Holy Spirit, who provides the power to "be."

ZONE DEFENSE

A study found that just a single moment of terror or rage consumes as much of the energy in the body as many hours of hard labor. You know how draining it can be when the negativity gets overwhelming. After people experience a big scare or become really angry, they feel tired. If they are bitter, angry people or just anxious worriers, they regularly consume the energy the body makes at a much faster rate and tend to be frequently tired. Parenting can be exhausting enough without this added drain.

Guarding against these enemy states of mind helps you stay in the zone as you face the unavoidable negative information, confrontations, and expectations. Remain in the super performance that only God can give by guarding your heart. As Proverbs 4:23 says, "Above all else, guard your heart, for everything you do flows from it."

Creative people and those who accomplish great exploits are said to operate at a level of only 10 percent above or even less than those who are just existing (just surviving). In other words, super performers practice, study, and in other ways prepare and perform at a level that is only 10 percent higher than the rest of us.

When you begin to walk in the provision of God's Spirit, parenting a special needs sweetheart, circumstances rarely stop tempting you to worry, fear, or get angry with someone or something. For this reason, it's important to guard against fear, anxiety, anger, and any other negative attitudes, including unforgiveness. They diminish both your performance and your energy to perform.

The enemies that drain us can keep us from our godly inheritance! Worrying is detrimental to inheriting God's promises. Forsaking anger is not only a godly response but also a healthy, empowering one. Learning to abide in the peace of God is so valuable. It suffocates the fire of irrational, emotional upheavals. Philippians 4:8 has the answer we need. It says, "Finally, brothers and sisters, whatever is true, whatever is noble, whatever is right, whatever is pure, whatever is lovely, whatever is admirable—if anything is excellent or praiseworthy—think about such things."

It is possible to experience His peace in the difficult times ahead and get into the courage zone. Resist fear. Resist anger. Forgive. Hit a home run out of the park! 2 Timothy 1:7 says, "For the Spirit God gave us does not make us timid, but gives us power, love and self-discipline." Choose the peace that surpasses understanding. Getting in the zone is a skill to master, yes, but not one you acquire on your own, God offers it to His team. And you are on His family team!

Guard Your Heart

Just as forgiveness serves endurance and diligence well,
peace fortifies against the onslaught of hell.

Every good answer may not cause desire to produce,
but every God answer bears eternal fruit. (2 Peter 1:11)

Love doesn't always say yes or offer a sweet caress. It sometimes curtails,
but no matter what it's called on to do, love never fails.

Offer spiritual sacrifices to God that are acceptable (1 Peter 2:5),
and remember a meek and quiet spirit is not only
precious but imperishable!
(1 Peter 3:4)

The courage zone for you is a God zone, a zone where fear of mistakes or assailing discomfort no longer dictate your responses. In that zone, your setbacks as a parent and as a person no longer have the power to define you. Nor do they dictate your score on the team.

PRACTICAL TIPS

Jana quoted Psalm 91 every morning while getting dressed. Her son continues to read the Psalm when he feels anxious. He loves music, so Jana bought him a keyboard. What a joy for her to see him stand and play for hours.

Keri discovered that if she kept soft, peaceful, instrumental music playing in her home day and night, it added a measure of tranquility.

John and Kathy were athletic runners. When they went for a good run, it aided their stress release and helped calm the parental rough roads.

Consider making your list of situations, thoughts, activities, people, and even your child's responses that give you peace.

PRAY

Dear Lord, until I see You face to face or in the answer that I seek, may I be found in Your abiding grace, my soul quieted by Your peace. Immerse me once again in the fullness of Your Spirit. Equip and empower me to live in and by the Holy Spirit. I trust You to grant me the courage required. Enable me be a tuned-in parent that is aware of my child's needs, approaches, and interactions. I trust I am growing in confidence. Thank you for the new techniques I am learning. I want to respond to every opportunity, making it a meaningful one. Help me rest in You and wait patiently. I believe the atmosphere in my home is loving, hopeful, and inwardly peaceful.

REFLECT

1. What does peace mean to you as a parent of a child with special needs? Consider releasing creative words based on God's words.

    - I can do all things through Christ who is strengthening me. (Philippians 4:13)
    - I am more than a conqueror in Christ Jesus.
      (Romans 8:37)
    - A spirit of fear no longer controls me, but I have a spirit of love, power, and self-discipline. I have a sound mind.
      (2 Timothy 1:7)
    - I live, move, and have my being in Christ. I trust in the Lord and the power of His might. My mind is set on what the Spirit desires.
      (Acts 17:28)

2. Consider writing down your own positive identity statements based on God's defining life-giving words, releasing the power of His Spirit to bring them to pass. Consider reading them often to strengthen your "courage zone" in Him.

5

Frozen Waterfalls: How Can I?

Guilty, defensive, and aloof to relieved, understanding, and equipped

YES, THE INITIAL sticker shock of what it would take to provide ongoing care for your child took your breath away. But you survived. You began your search for how to live in your *transitioning identity*. But at times, harsh, cold circumstances can pile one on top of the other. You can feel as if your soul has begun to freeze over, much like a frozen waterfall—immobilized. What happened to the flow of power and blessing?

Your plans for the future have come to a standstill. You live in a different (or is *alien* a better word?) world than almost everyone you know. The caring and love of friends and family do not seem to make the needed difference.

Waterfalls are one of nature's marvels. Most likely you've stood transfixed by falling water at one time or another, paused to listen to a trickling fall, or even hiked somewhere remote to marvel over the power of world famous falls such as Niagara or Victoria Falls. But what about a frozen waterfall? Have you stared at one, listening for the frozen voice? Can you relate right now to its frozen state?

John recalls the initial shock, but there seemed to be a healthy ability to hope for the best. He believed things were going to work out. Then as one difficulty seemed to lead into another, the overwhelmed, fixed stare came over his face more often. He began to feel like his hope had been premature and he was being slowly drained of any sense of ability to cope. He said, "Through it all, I discovered a different me, a me I didn't know existed. Sometimes it was a me I never wanted to experience again, but in time it was a better me, a resilient man who not only could cope, but enjoy life in the journey."

What kind of force causes a cascading waterfall to freeze in motion? Unlike what happens with still bodies of water, the physics of freezing is a lot more complicated with moving water. Waterfalls don't immediately stop flowing and freeze over when the temperature plummets to freezing point. Time is required for any noticeable change of state compared with still water under the same conditions. In a free-falling waterfall, ice begins by clinging to an overhang. Gradually the ice forms an anchor from which it can grow. If the water is sufficiently cold enough, for long enough, a column grows that eventually runs the length of the waterfall.

The freeze for parents gradually begins in the surviving stage when it dawns on them what they are actually facing. While searching for answers, they look inward as well as outward. It could be they are angry with themselves for birthing or adopting their child. Some carry the deep, all-encompassing pain of knowing that they or the birth parents made a poor choice that led to their child's special needs. Any continual disappointment can create a soul-ravaging condition for ice to attach. They can begin to freeze inside.

ICY SILENCE

After the initial months of struggle and necessary adaptations of the survival stage, followed by the exhausting search stage, many parents feel isolated and alone, punctuated with days when they can barely move. They find it difficult to believe they will ever feel "normal" again. What is normal anyway? A common response, when someone reaches out, is sometimes just one of those lost-in-the-arctic stares or a faint voice response, "I don't want to talk about it." Too frozen for words.

"I kept it all to myself," shared John. "No one at work knew the full measure of what my family was handling with our newborn. We didn't even tell the relatives back East. It seemed more energy consuming than it was worth to try and explain. Who could understand our pain anyway? And, to be honest, we didn't know for sure if we were to blame. Silence seemed like the best choice."

Denette describes a milestone day in her situation as the foster parent and then adopted parent of a child with special needs.

Therapy with a 2 x 4?

> My foster child, Bill, and I were in infant stimulation one day when the abusive birth parents walked in. My husband and I were so angry. We weren't supposed to see them or they us. We knew they were in therapy. When my husband saw them, he said he would like to give them therapy with a 2 by 4 for what they did to this baby.
>
> When I saw them that day, they asked if I was the foster parent. As I looked at them, answering their question, a different emotion came over me. They were more pitiful than the horrible people I had made imagined. The birth mother had a younger brother that had been killed by abuse, and her father was in prison for manslaughter. The birth mother had come to the conclusion that when people looked at her son, she and her husband's abuse and shameful ways would be exposed. Therefore, she "released" him to us for adoption.
>
> My sister, Carole, asked me later, "How did you move from angry retaliation thoughts to sympathy for them?"
>
> "It was God, only God," I answered. "It took time, but as our love for Bill grew, our compassion for his parents began to override the anger. We felt sorry for them and began to pray that their therapy times would bring healthy restoration."

You may have experienced similar emotions as Denette and her husband. Or you may wonder how long you will experience the icy anger. Maybe you wonder if, or even know, actions of yours contributed to your child's special needs. The ice has begun to form on the overhang in your heart. How long will you suffer cold, painful regret or guilty anguish?

If you believe or know you were at fault for your child's condition, your reactions to certain circumstances (you know them) can contribute to the ice that is building inside. They can cause you to feel guilt or shame, fear, anger, or even unidentified emotional pain accompanied by the self-hatred that produces sheer exhaustion.

The shame of wondering. Was it something I ingested into my body? Did I leave out some critical vitamin? Am I the guilty one? Could my child's condition have been in the family line DNA? These questions and more can freeze your emotions.

The feeling of fear. What else? How much more? Will something happen in the middle of the night that I just can't handle? Is my child going to live a full life? What will schooling be like next year? Do I have enough money to deal with all the health and care needs ahead? How will my marriage be affected?

The experience of exhaustion. I can't take it any more. I can't earn enough money to meet bills. If I can't get a grip on my situation, others will brand me with being unfit, uncaring, unable. I don't know how I can go on anymore. My self-deprecating words and thoughts are offensive even to me, deepening my sense of inability and robbing me of potential for victory.

The *settling* stage just ahead is a sorting and shifting time. It's also a time to remember the resource you have for your soul health: Christ Jesus as your personal Lord and the Holy Spirit your Comforter. You and your family are precious in His sight. The Holy Spirit knows what no one person can fully grasp and can go where no human can go. He can make the difference. He can bring newness of life for you. Relief is coming, whether understanding fills in the blanks of your questions or not.

Regardless of how you got here, awareness of the honor afforded you in this parenting journey is learned, and anything that is learned takes time. Give both yourself and those around you time to come to more positive, encouraging conclusions of who you are, what you can do, and how you are going to experience God's prevailing love and peace. Continue to give time and a listening ear to the Spirit of God. With His help, quietness can outweigh the internal questioning. It's a supernatural, miraculous truth that anger, guilt, shame, regret, and the negative effects of the physical and emotional hard labor you are experiencing or have experienced can be overcome.

Every child is a gift. The activity of being a parent of a child with unique needs can turn into a surprising adventure, like the Alaskan cruise that replaced the planned tropical island vacation. Parenting a child with special needs becomes an opportunity to live out an expression of unconditional love in ways that few will ever have the privilege to experience. Whether your emotions validate the truth or not, it's an honor to be entrusted with your child—to be the parent.

ICE ANCHOR

When you think of a frozen waterfall, words such as *immobilized, suspended*, or *unfriendly* might come to mind. Do you know people who actually climb these gigantic, frozen masterpieces of beauty? Frozen waterfall climbing is an advanced form of ice climbing. Have you ever glanced through ice climbing magazines or scanned climbers' websites? The photographs are incredible. There they are, those wild-hearted men and women, scaling frozen waterfalls. It makes you wonder what inspires and enables them.

Ice climbers, those who scale the frozen walls, do so with a bag of tools. The most important tools are the pick and the anchor. The pick creates an opening where there was none, and the anchor holds them safely in place until the next step can be taken.

Here are three Scripture verses for your "tool bag" with some ax and anchor words (inserts in parentheses mine).

> "For the word of God is living and active, sharper than any double-edged sword (*or a pick axe*), it penetrates even to dividing soul and spirit, joints and marrow; it judges the thoughts and attitudes of the

heart. Nothing in all creation is hidden from God's sight" (Hebrews 4:12–13).

"Therefore my dear brothers and sisters, stand firm. Let nothing move you (*stay anchored*). Always give yourselves fully to the work of the Lord, because you know that your labor in the Lord is not in vain" (1 Corinthians 15:58).

"We have this hope as an anchor for the soul, firm and secure" (Hebrews 6:19).

The experienced ice climber gathers his tools and uses them with skill to climb from the bottom of the frozen falls to the top. You are gathering tools for the climb. The more you use them, the more skilled you will become. But before you can move forward in the *settling* stage, where ice climbing doesn't seem too crazy after all. Letting go of guilt or offense and gaining the emotional and spiritual skill of forgiveness is foundational.

GUILT

Every parent deals with guilt. Angie's story is an example. A second-time mother, Angie was fairly confident in her parenting skills. One day as she rushed up the stairs with her six-month-old to change a dirty diaper, she tripped and fell on the stairs. Her arms took the brunt of the fall, but to her dismay, her baby's forehead hit the stair step as well. Horrified, Angie watched as a thin line of blood began to form on her daughter's face. Soon it was apparent that a stitch or two would have to be made to close the wound.

When Angie arrived at the hospital, she was filled with guilt. How could she have been so careless? Would her daughter's face bear a scar for the rest of her life, reminding Angie of her mistake? Worse yet, would the bump lead to a traumatic brain injury? The hospital staff made Angie repeat the story of the fall again and again to different individuals, one a social worker who implied not so indirectly that the story Angie told was not true, that perhaps child abuse was involved. Horror was added to Angie's guilt when she realized the implication.

At first Angie was frozen. Who knew where this icy storm she was in would lead? She was certainly guilty of causing a serious injury to her baby, but it had been an accident. Those wooden steps should have been covered with carpet. She wasn't the only one at fault. As her daughter's stitches healed, Angie watched anxiously for signs of brain trauma. And as she watched, she prayed, asking God for His forgiveness and healing.

Family and friends were aghast at the situation, but Angie anchored herself in God. The wound healed. The scar was minor. Years later, her daughter did struggle in school and was diagnosed as having a mild learning disability. With help, she overcame her limitations and went on to earn her MBA and become a successful businesswoman and mother. Did the fall cause the learning disability, or was it in her daughter's DNA all along? Angie will never know.

Family members other than parents can suffer from guilt. Camille's story that follows shows how siblings can suffer as well.

The Big Sister

While it may not seem logical, guilt is a very big by-product for the sibling of a disabled individual. Ask any of us.

As the older sister of a severely disabled brother with cerebral palsy, I have grown up feeling helpless, guilty, and in a constant state of searching for answers to the deepest mysteries of life. With no authority to be a decision-maker in my brother's life, I had no choice but to be a frustrated observer as my parents called all the shots for life decisions for my sweet yet helpless brother.

Kevin is without the ability to control ANY of his motor functions except his beautiful eyes and smile. Standing by as a protective big sister, watching him grow up and being unable to "fix him," I am in a constant state of discontentment and restlessness. Not a day goes by without a deep, dull ache in my soul because I am able to live a "normal" life while my own flesh-and-blood brother is locked into a body that does not work.

> For much of my life, I have been in the searching stage and not really able to move past it. Part of the reason is that I have had no control over big decisions—putting him in a full-time institution at age three, not giving him resources to stimulate his brain and body at a young age, and putting him on a G-tube because of the risks of pneumonia. But the larger cause is that I have questioned God.
>
> My journey to understand the mind of God on the ultimate stumper question of "why" has propelled me to press into the pain and discover more and more that the only satisfying answers lie with the knowledge of God. I have discovered that for me the only exit from the searching stage is to press deeper into the knowledge of God. Only He has the answers that satisfy my soul, because only HE offers hope beyond this world at the same time that He offers peace in this world through the peace He brings to my heart.

Whether guilt is warranted or unwarranted, it is important to overcome it. A guilty parent or a parent holding a grudge against someone else's guilt isn't free to become the parent he or she longs to be. Guilt hinders the healthy *settling in* stage.

FORGIVENESS

Have you ever lived in a climate of cold and harsh weather, with frequent icy rains or blizzard snows? How much travel can be accomplished in those weather conditions? Very little if any at all. Visibility is reduced at best, and sometimes you are hopelessly iced or snowed in.

Unforgiveness is like bad weather. It stops the free flow of God's blessings. Unforgiveness toward yourself or others holds you captive with reoccurring thoughts of bitterness, disappointment, and pain. It has a negative spiritual, emotional, and physical effect on your whole being. It blocks God's best entrance for comfort and help. You can end up feeling like an Alaskan tree frog in the winter when two-thirds of its body's water freezes to the point it is almost like a frogsicle.

Denise was familiar with the freezing cold of unforgiveness. "I can't tell you the number of times I blew it!" she lamented. "My stomach would turn every time I heard the voicemails from the therapist asking for another time alone with me or my workmate telling me I had a phone call from school again. And the worst angry reactions came when my son forcibly refused to take his meds or be strapped in his seat. I resented them all for making my life so miserable, or at least that was what I was thinking at the time.

"Finally forgiveness became my antifreeze. I learned that forgiveness isn't about letting yourself or someone get away with wrongdoing. It's about being released from the emotional and spiritual consequences, leaving the outcome to God. Over and over Luke 6:37, 'Forgive, and you will be forgiven,' came to mind, and with it a fresh ability to release myself and those I held offense against."

Her story brings to mind the words of Acts 3:19. "Repent, then, and turn to God, so that your sins may be wiped out, that times of refreshing may come from the Lord." The word *repent* simply means to change your mind and act another way.

Ron said he and his wife blamed themselves after they discovered their blind daughter suffered from a genetic disease. They considered it their fault. Self-forgiveness was paramount in their ability to move forward.

Josh learned the relationship of forgiveness to guilt, pain, and negative emotions such as anger. "Less guilt equals less pain; less anger, less pain. Yes, it's good to reassess yourself or the advice of the professionals you are confiding in. When appropriate, make the needed adjustments. Then, after you have done so, give yourself an emotional and spiritual respite. Forgive."

Jana, mother of a child born with hydrocephalus, found forgiveness to be a challenge.

Forgiving the Unforgiveable

At three months of pregnancy, I thought I was going to lose my child. I prayed a simple prayer, and the symptoms lessened. All was well, or so I thought.

Jason had a traumatic birth. He was born C-section after fifty-two hours of labor. After a week in the hospital, he began to show signs of a problem. Nothing would soothe his crying. He was continually upset. Doctors, however, said everything was fine.

We, the patients and parents, have a tendency to believe doctors have all the answers. In this case, my husband and I chose to get another opinion. We took Jason to another town, and another diagnosis came: hydrocephalus with only hours to live. Suddenly it was life or death. Necessary treatment was given.

Needless to say, when the crisis was averted and we could think again, we had to do some serious forgiving towards the doctors in the small town where we lived. They did not have the knowledge to diagnose and would have just let him die.

NEVERTHELESS

You may have professionals you consulted with in the past that you have held captive in offense, or you may feel like you deserve what pain comes your way. It is possible that you believe God's loving forgiveness is a wonderful offer but still have trouble grasping it. Why? Could it be you don't think you deserve it? Nevertheless, He forgives you.

Shaunie struggled with self-forgiveness. She wrote the following in her journal.

Frozen Waterfalls, Frogsicles, and Me

Too little energy to move.
Deep cold is setting in.
Will I feel warmth again?
What is stopping me?
Can I be an anomaly?
Even frozen Alaskan tree frogs live.
Frozen waterfalls cascade over the edge.
There must be hope for me.
Subzero temperatures! What are they to You?
Surely there's antifreeze for my soul.
In the meantime I want to be a champion of the cold.
Revive my heart.
Give me breath.
Make me mysteriously bold.

Shaunie understands the frozen state of being unable to forgive herself. "I learned the hard way that self-unforgiveness results in shame, and shame is one of the hardest strongholds to defeat. It debilitates who you believe you can become, and it disables any form of confidence or boldness. One day I found myself staring at the closet for an hour because I didn't want to make a bad decision. And what was the decision that was so immobilizing? It was only choosing what to wear for the day!"

Thankfully others were there to help her. "At first it was impossible to believe that I should be forgiven. Even when I wanted to believe, I couldn't. It took people forgiving me, showing me unconditional love, before I could fathom believing I could be free from shame."

Forgiving yourself is paramount in responding to the price Jesus paid to forgive, redeem, and restore you. It's not a feeling. It's an act of faith. It's a choice of your will to come into agreement with God's merciful love. Self-forgiveness melts your hardened heart and releases your emotions to experience healthy relational interchanges once again.

Forgiveness gets even better with time. It restores a warm, delightful, sunshiny disposition. It counteracts the harsh, fierce cold. Mercy, a companion of forgiveness, is catalytic and possesses a wonderful kind of elasticity. It bounces back to all those who choose to extend it. Matthew 5:7 says, "Blessed are the merciful, for they will be shown mercy." This Scripture verse makes it clear that it is to the merciful that God will extend His mercy in return. Take a deep breath. Choose to release any offense as you breath out. Now receive forgiveness where needed as you slowly breath in and out a few times. Can you feel mercy's relief melting away the unwanted?

When the world's political hero from South Africa, Nelson Mandela, died in December of 2013, several newscasters repeated his most profound, iconic statements. He'd had a strong influence in the country even while he was in prison. Rather than pursue vengeance against his opposition after serving twenty-seven years in prison, he chose to forgive and move on. When he was freed and became president of South Africa, his words flowed freely in the opposite spirit of what he had personally experienced. The effect was transforming. His leadership of the country became an example of this truth: "Forgiveness has the power to heal."

Mandela did not ask the questions "Who me?" or "Why me?" or "How can . . . ?" Because he didn't, his nationwide influence was strong even while incarcerated. His questions, instead, were, "What's next?" and "What do we need to do now that will accomplish the goal, making the historic difference?" His open forgiveness shone bright throughout the country of South Africa. When he was released from prison, he was elected to the highest position of leadership in the nation.

Sun can melt ice. Frozen waterfalls can thaw in the warmth of the sunshine. But until the water's rushing forces crash over the edge of the cliff once again, the adventurous ice climbers can take on the challenge. They don't forget the inviting magnificent view from the top.

A forgiven person, one who welcomes God's cleansing, is open to a daring attitude about parenting and new altitudes in the parenting climb. Your heart is what changes when you receive the fullness of His forgiveness for yourself and toward others. And when your heart changes, hope emerges. Colors are brighter. The daily, grinding schedule loses a bit of its rough edges. Relationships aren't as strained. Emotional energy resurfaces. You feel a strong sense of internal freedom. You discover an inward grin, a healthy gratitude for the little blessings you hadn't noticed along the way. The freedom is exhilarating.

1 John 1:9 says, "But if we confess our sins to him, he can be depended on to forgive us and to cleanse us from every wrong." John 20:23 says, "If you forgive anyone's sins, their sins are forgiven."

Greater

Whose sin is greater than His purity?
Whose unbelief can cancel His grace?
Whose tradition can alter any of His virtue?
Not mine.
Not mine.

Whose storm can overtake His peace?
Whose fear can constrain His reigning glory?
Whose ignorance can swallow up His mercy?
Not mine.
Not mine.

His life is everlasting, enduring love until my very end!
His goodness proclaims His favor, driving out darkness for all time!
His Name is Jesus Christ, Son of God, Savior, Lord, and my Friend.
All mine!
All mine!

The source of this "nevertheless" way of thinking is revealed in the story recorded in Luke 7:36–50. Jesus tells a story to explain why a tearful woman ignored the judgmental rejection by the leaders of the day. She, pressing past them, reverently anointed Jesus with expensive perfumed oil. "Therefore, I tell you, her many sins have been forgiven—as her great love has shown. But whoever has been forgiven little loves little" (Luke 7:47). Knowing you are forgiven and forgiving others flings open the door to experience empowering love at its finest.

Forgiveness is flowing. Love is fulfilling. God's expensive and expansive love has forgiven you. You can now extend His merciful forgiveness to those in critical need of someone to forgive them (Matthew 6:12). God doesn't want you frozen, ravaged by disappointment, helpless, desperate, cold hearted, or immovable. As you release the hard feelings you have harbored against yourself or others, a fresh, invigorating strength helps you perceive what steps to take next as you climb.

Mercy

Mercy's obtaining price shall ever remain the same.
"Give me away," she cries,
"and proclaim Jesus' holy name."
When you thrust through mercy's side,
no violation can abide.
From her fountain flows love's release,
and in her bounty all sin does cease.
"If you love me less,
shall I not love you more?
Shall I do despite unto the Spirit of Grace (Hebrews 10:29)
And the stripes Jesus bore?"
No, mercy honors grace
and pays the tribute that is due.
So heart, be enlarged toward yourself and others.
Please the One who is Faithful and True.

You are beginning to realize your heavenly Father is not the author of the negative parental situations you face but instead the author of your upcoming wisdom, comfort, and strength. He is equipping you with what you need to climb to the heights of the frozen waterfall.

Your capacity to love is increasing. God's graciousness, mercy, and love have granted you a heart of compassion toward others as you choose to act on His truths with a whole heart (Luke 6:36). 1 John 1:7 says, "If we walk in the light, as he is in the light, we have fellowship with one another, and the blood of Jesus, his Son, purifies us from all sin." 2 Corinthians 4:6 says, "For God, who said, 'Let light shine out of darkness,' made his light shine in our hearts to give us the light of the knowledge of God's glory displayed in the face of Christ."

Your heavenly Father is always about increase. You've asked for forgiveness, and you have forgiven. You have extended mercy, which is His mercy. His light is shining where darkness once prevailed. His gift is the light of the knowledge of the glory of God in the face of Christ.

PRAY

Dear Lord Jesus, I am so thankful for the sacrifice of Your love that forgives me of my sin. It is written in 1 John 1:9 that if I confess my sins, You are faithful and just to forgive them. Today I bring the smallest to the greatest before you and ask for Your forgiveness. I choose to forgive not only those who have sinned against my family or me but also to forgive myself.

Also in 1 John 1:9, You said that You would cleanse me of all unrighteousness when I ask forgiveness. I trust You to not only forgive me but to cleanse me of all the reasons I missed the mark, blew past the stop signs, chose wrongly or ran in the wrong direction. I choose today to turn around and believe You have forgiven me, delivered me, cleansed me, and given me the fullness of Your Holy Spirit to flood all those places, once bound by sin, as You make clean my inward being.

Father God, while I am waiting for the full intensity of the sunlight of Your love to melt those frozen places, I trust I am discovering new ice-climbing skills. I believe one day I'll look up and realize the season for ice climbing is over. The falls are flowing again, the sun is shining, and it is time to move on to the next adventure.

REFLECT

1. Who is exasperating you, offending you, abandoning you, or just plain irritating you? Consider saying a prayer of forgiveness for the ones coming to your mind as you were reading.

2. Now consider taking a step further. Bless them with a caring thought in prayer. You could ask God to comfort, support, or generally bless their family or work. You could pray for their eternal relationship with Jesus to be close and dynamic. There are so many ways to bless those who persecute you or pray for those who despitefully use you as well as those that just get in the way. Consider saying an inward prayer each time you find yourself feeling or thinking a negative thought about them. You will be responding

in the opposite spirit of your past inclinations, and very likely it will be more healthy for you personally.

3. Forgiveness both protects and provides for your own soul. Deep breath, let go of self unforgiveness and receive God's mercy enabling you to be restored.

6

Faith Lifts: What's Different?

Dread, mental gymnastics, and exhaustion to renewal, calm decision-making, and rest

The sheer weight of responsibilities, continually trying to fix what can't be fixed and maniacally focusing on nagging details, added to lack of sleep, can induce those pesky stress chemicals that zap emotional and physical stability. The mixture is a concoction for sheer exhaustion. And it's true for any parent, especially if there is more than one small child in a family.

Consider the counsel in Isaiah 40:31. "Those who hope in the Lord will renew their strength. They will soar on wings like eagles; they will run and not grow weary, they will walk and not be faint."

When you move out of the sticker-shock-surviving and desperately-searching-for-answers stages, you begin to experience a greater measure of faith-born settling-in peace. Well, at least more than when your child was first diagnosed. You aren't as beaten down by the onslaught of problems, multitudes of doctor appointments, and family trials. Even the extra physical work seems lighter somehow. Your poise under pressure has increased to some degree.

You're acquiring serenity both from experience and a gift of grace. Something in you has changed, and it is making a difference.

Your daily routine probably hasn't become everything rest has to offer yet, but your prayers are morphing hopefully from desperation into more awareness of the Holy Spirit's gentle presence. The challenges may not have changed, but hints of expectancy are seeping in. Your internal story can hum a lighthearted tune. You are beginning to identify the Holy Spirit's willingness to comfort, guide, and support. When you find yourself wondering what's next, overwhelming dread of what might lie ahead no longer has the power to usurp your whole day, trying to control panic. You're definitely moving forward with a greater ease.

SETTLING

Settling, the third stage of transformation, starts when you begin choosing your battles and balancing your child's special needs with the schedules and demands of other family members. It continues much longer and is much more peaceful than the early times of surviving and searching. It is the practical, experiential part of your parenting journey. As you settle in, your searching either culminates with acceptance of how things are or, at the least, becomes somewhat less aggressive in the drive for answers. Emotional responses are less frantic than before. That's a relief!

In this stage, your pace of living is steadier, perhaps slower. You feel more resilient and less a victim of circumstances. You are gathering a network of resources for help (at least for the present round of issues). Triumphs don't come by just getting through a day because you are beginning to have a renewed sense of confidence in how you will manage the days ahead.

Remember how Gideon, the unlikely hero in the book of Judges, handled continual hardship? At first he wondered where this wondrous God had been and if He really loved him and his people. He was convinced God had abandoned them. He kept asking God to show Himself strong while taking one more step until the Spirit of God transformed him into the man we read about today. In the *surviving* and *searching* stages, God had to remind, even command Gideon, to fear not and be at peace. God's command wasn't a fierce demand but instead one empowered with grace that enabled Gideon to rise in courage while still feeling unsafe and fearful. As he began to settle into his new role with a firmer grasp of his identity, life became more confident, with times of God-given boldness and daring faith.

As Gideon moved further into his *settling* stage, he had a revelation of God's powerful presence with him. Chapter 6 of Judges records his shock and surprise. "When Gideon realized that it was the angel of the LORD, he exclaimed, 'Alas, sovereign LORD! I have seen the angel of the LORD face to face'" (v. 22). Gideon went from fear of death and being commanded to be at peace to realizing he wasn't going to have to do this assignment from the Lord alone. God was not asking him to muster up faith and power. Instead, his heavenly Father was there to work the work of the Kingdom in and through him. He progressed even further by declaring his deep revelation that the Lord Himself is peace (v. 24).

See how Matt's family fared at this stage by getting creative in managing their life within the limitations of Duchenne's.

Getting Creative

It seemed like everything would be going along smoothly, and then something major would happen in Matt's health, or the insurance company said it wasn't going to take care of one of the bills for Matt. Accurate or not, it seemed like every six months something would change.

As a family we tried our best to take everything in stride and be as normal as can be, whatever that meant for a family with a special needs child. We went skiing. Matt did too. When we went hiking, we would put him in an umbrella stroller and carry it up the path when the trail became steep or rocky. He could swim like a fish, or rather bobbed up and down, but when he was in the water he could move his arms and legs and felt free. These times were wonderful and peaceful.

I remember one time going up to Mammoth Lakes to stay. The place had a ping pong table, and Matt wanted to play. We had a table at

> home, so we designed a hat with a shield in front so he could hit the ball off of the shield along with the paddle. Another time we found a way to play tennis. Since Matt didn't have upper body strength, we put the racket on his chair so he could move the chair and hit the ball.
>
> Matt loved sports. In high school he was required to take physical education class. Even though he couldn't play, the football coach allowed him to be on the football team, down on the field during the games. This provision fulfilled his requirement for graduation. He even became the senior editor for his high school newspaper and wrote a weekly article for it.
>
> Matt didn't see himself as being disabled and wanted only to be treated like everyone else. He went to the movies often and loved to eat out. Cruising the mall and checking out the girls was a favorite time for him.

It's common to feel weak and unprepared at first. There's nothing new there for all parents! The good news is what can come next—creative ideas. The Brown family was vigilant in their pursuit of creative expressions of life for Matt no matter what hardship came his way. They did not let go of their faith that God Himself was providing the internal, prevailing peace that supersedes understanding.

SETTLED PEACE WITH NEWFOUND FAITH

Have you learned to drive a vehicle with a stick shift? At first it takes full concentration. Jerky movements. Grinding gears. Stalls. Exasperated driver and passengers. But after a while of trial and error, you find your way. You shift easily through the gears. You and your passengers hardly even notice the movements.

God has and will continue to work a shifting ease within you. It's often unexplainable, a conundrum, a mystery. As you practice shifting your concerns His way, you will discover a greater capacity for His presence and trust in His workmanship for your family. His gifts can show up at surprising times. You will increase in your ability to handle more. It won't be nearly as taxing on your body or soul as it once was. His faith will lift you. You will be elevated higher and higher. A settled peace will lift you above the cloud cover. There will be an atmospheric change. His loving care and merciful guidance will make the difference.

A few years ago Hollywood offered a movie entitled *Hope Floats.* Doesn't just reading the title lift expectations and deposit a hopeful, settling effect on your soul? Faith is the substance of things hoped for, says Hebrews 11:1. You may not have broken through the cloud cover yet, but you are close and you know it. Don't you love the word *yet?* You know life will never be the same, and yet you have uncovered reasons to smile and maybe even have outlandish bursts of joy. Hope is beginning to "float" for you.

Where did the new sense of hope come from? And faith? Or is it faith? If faith, in what? If not, what else could it be?

Faith is not some abstract, ethereal, mystic awareness. It has solid substance and inherent, metamorphic power when its source is the Creator of the Universe. Faith that results in powerful, "mighty warrior" living is faith that centers itself on a powerful God in the person of Jesus Christ.

Faith is an invitation into a renewed mind. In contrast to frantic reactions, faith's progressive working in your soul will enable you to more easily process information, no longer leaning on what you can understand alone, but instead recognizing that God's love and faithfulness will never leave you. Give Him time.

When you realize faith has already taken up residence in your spirit, in spite of the various needs you and your family may be facing, you are empowered to choose to "in all your ways submit to him" (Proverbs 3:6). It's a reality that enables you to take your eyes off both you and your child's personal weaknesses and gaze implicitly on God's ability to make a way where there was no way to meet your needs. Faith lifts. Hope gives you confident buoyancy.

"Faith, why are you there?" you may ask. "I am the evidence of what you cannot yet see," faith whispers in reply.

Does it make sense? Does it have to? Not today. It's enough to know that faith is there, collaborating with hope and steadily moving you toward emergence. You see its evidence when you begin to hear yourself expressing a more tranquil reaction to settings. The wisdom, peace, and sense of stability you feel at times are surprising. You look at yourself in the mirror and ask, "Where did that come from?" It's happening. You are becoming supernaturally natural!

Faith

Faith makes the outlook calm,
the uplook constant,
the inlook accurate.

Faith makes yesterday a stepping stone,
today a limitless possibility,
and tomorrow a gift of joy!

MANAGING STRESS

A healthy two-year-old with strong legs can be dangerous. Gail's little boy was swifter than a puma. The second he saw the door open, half dressed, he would bolt past his mom and run for the street as fast as his little legs could carry him before Gail could grab him. She would then have to stop everything and swiftly fly through the door, chasing after her runaway darling.

One morning, nine months pregnant with her second child, Gail went outside to get the newspaper. Her little boy saw an opportune moment and pulled his sneaky maneuver, dashing through the crack in the door behind her. She hadn't dressed yet except for an old robe that didn't quite surround her now bulging-with-new-baby middle. No time to think about it. She grabbed each side of the robe and took off running barefoot down the street. Winded and furious by the time she caught up with him, she grabbed his arm, scooped him up, and took him home.

Your thoughts can run just as fast. The nagging, practical, daily demands of your life can "stress open" the door for your mind to run as fast as it can into negative, debilitating thinking. It happens. But fear not. You haven't lost your faith. Chase down your thinking as Gail did her son. Bring it back where it belongs—into the safety and security of home where hope, your growing faith, and love can oversee, guard, and discipline its ways.

Caroline Leaf, a brain scientist and author of *Who Switched Off My Brain,* says, "Stress is the direct result of toxic thinking. . . . When you are under extreme stress, chemicals flood your body and create physical effects caused by intense feelings. When those feelings are, for example, anger, fear, anxiety or bitterness, the effects on your health are nothing short of horrific in the long term." She also says, "Although you may not be able to control your environment all of the time, you can control how it affects your brain."

Dr. Leaf's Web post of May 23, 2014 (http://drleaf.com/blog/positive-versus-negative-stress/) reads, "Stress is a backup system in the body designed to help us focus, cope and rejoice despite the circumstances! However, incorrect reactions turn stress from being a 'backup' system to a 'breakup' system." Leaf assures readers that they can free themselves from toxic thinking. "As toxic thoughts are swept away, they will be replaced with the foundation for health and peace."

Your thoughts can sweep away unhealthy stress chemicals, making you more clever and calm, subduing any damaging emotions, or they can do just the opposite. If not today, there will come a day when you will be able to come into agreement with hope and faith. Your thinking will be enabled to choose! Leaf implicitly states that bathing in positive environments will enable your intellect to flourish and with it, your mental and physical health. Your day is coming.

ROCK CLIMBING

You are beginning to discover the benefits of throwing all your weight on the faithfulness of your heavenly Father. Maybe it would be a good time for a faith act.

What is a faith act? It's when you do something to illustrate what you believe no matter how ravaged your soul may feel. Here's just one example. You might go to your bed and with your whole body, just melt into the mattress for a few minutes as you whisper thoughts to your heavenly Father, casting all your care on Him.

Rock climbing is an activity in which people climb up, down, or across natural rock formations. The goal is to reach the summit of a formation or the endpoint of a predefined route. Rock climbers have equipment and strategies that enable them to climb the heights, not unlike the ice climbers mentioned earlier. But they too need to rest.

God can create a cliff cabana for your soul like the ones rock climbers use on their extreme journeys. Imagine one of those mountaineering triangular tents that hang from a mountain ledge or tree for the night so the weary climber can rest. You can rest in one of those too, anchored on the mountainside by your heavenly Father. Now that really would be a new adventure!

Faith's climbing gear is not earned through your own efforts. It is given to you when you trust. It includes the spiritual climbing rope, cord, webbing, harness, rappel devices, ascenders, slings, protection devices, training equipment, specialized clothing, quick draws, and carabineers you need for the climb. It includes everything right down to the little items like tape and a bear sling or haul bag—all the equipment of faith.

Great climbs require faith and faith's equipment. God's mercy grants you undeserved favor while His grace gives you His redeeming enablement. Sometimes God's provisions come directly to you, and other times they come from Him through a friend or family member standing in the gap for you in assistance, caring, faith, or prayer.

With all of these God-given provisions, you can rise to the heights. You can rest in a cliff cabana. The view from the top is worth the climb.

The apostle Paul comprehends the mystery of faith, and what a mystery it is. He writes his prayerful exhortation to the people in Ephesians 3:14–21 (MSG).

> My response is to get down on my knees before the Father, this magnificent Father who parcels out all heaven and earth. I ask him to strengthen you by his Spirit—not a brute strength but a glorious inner

> strength—that Christ will live in you as you open the door and invite him in. And I ask him that with both feet planted firmly on love, you'll be able to take in with all followers of Jesus the extravagant dimensions of Christ's love. Reach out and experience the breadth! Test its length! Plumb the depths! Rise to the heights! Live full lives, full in the fullness of God.

Rest is important to a successful climb. It can be a lengthy climb where great endurance is required. Regular rest becomes critical for the journey. Most people know that accidents or bad decisions can start happening if they become overly tired. When it happens, who doesn't want a safe return to home base?

You are a faith mountaineer, a rocky cliff climber. Your daily routine may be as physically and mentally demanding as any climber. Strength, endurance, agility, and balance are tested along with mental control. Be inspired by Sandra's willingness to go beyond what anyone would expect and her patience in the journey.

Sandra's Climb

> After successfully raising four boys (my measurement for success was that no one had been arrested or ended up in jail), we were facing an empty nest. Unable to have any more children, we decided to adopt. We discovered, however, that the only type of child we would qualify for was a child with a disability. How ironic to hope and pray through four pregnancies for a "normal, healthy baby" and then find ourselves in deep discussions regarding what sorts of disabilities we felt we were "qualified" to handle.
>
> After a couple of years of effort, disappointment, frustration, and tears, a tiny baby girl was placed into our arms by a Christian foster family who would become lifelong friends. The baby had been declared "medically healthy" by a renowned pediatrician, but because she was not doing the things a typical three-month old would do, she was classified as an "at risk" child. Twenty-four hours after bringing her home,

our own small-town pediatrician diagnosed a "probable syndrome" and referred us to a geneticist, who later confirmed the diagnosis of Fetal Alcohol Syndrome. It was one of the disabilities that we had thought we could NOT deal with. (God does work in mysterious ways!)

Our baby was affected cognitively and developmentally. The following years were filled with struggle, prayers, divine appointments, connections, trials, and triumphs. God stretched our faith in ways we could not have imagined, and He showed up in miracles, both big and small. One example was when a group of young girls in a local church adopted our daughter as their "prayer baby." Their childlike faith and prayers were answered by seeing a baby who was not expected to walk, or talk, take her first steps at age two and begin to use sign language at age four.

God arranged relationships with pioneer researchers, therapists on the cutting edge of working with infants, and people who came alongside of us to create pilot programs and help pass new legislation for birth to age three programs. Today our daughter is a 26-year-old young woman who loves meteorology and computers.

God eventually brought two more special needs children to our family. Each challenge we faced was an opportunity for God to lead, teach, guide, and bless us!

Mountaineering can be dangerous. Knowledge of climbing techniques and usage of specialized climbing equipment is crucial for the safe completion of routes. Its challenges are not unlike the quest of loving parents like you who are serving children with special needs. You begin your faith climb as a parent of a special needs child with little or no prior knowledge or skills to equip you. Gradually you get a good grasp on what equipment is needed to help you and your child. What local services are available? Who you can trust? How you can balance the hard work with quiet resting times. Questions answered (at least in part for now) and equipment at hand, you begin your climb.

Never forget, as you climb, that Jesus sent the Holy Spirit to be with you. He is the lifter of your head. Psalm 3:3 declares, "But you, LORD, are a shield around me, my glory, the One who lifts my head high." Climb with him, and at the end of each day, snuggle up to Him in your cliff cabana resting place. "Casting the whole of your care [all your anxieties, all your worries, all your concerns, once and for all] on Him, for He cares for you affectionately and cares about you watchfully" (1 Peter 5:7 AMP). Throw forcefully your care on Him. Trust Him.

Faith Mountaineer

I don't mean to complain, but it's a rocky mountain in a tough terrain.
Steep face, jagged rocks.
How am I supposed to get to the top?
Just climb. One step at a time.

Moses was a mountain climber. He followed God to the top of a mountain. "The Lord descended to the top of Mount Sinai and called Moses to the top of the mountain. So Moses went up" (Exodus 19:20). "The Lord said to Moses, 'Come up to me on the mountain and stay here, and I will give you the tablets of stone with the law and commands I have written for their instruction'" (Exodus 24:12).

When he came down from the climb, Moses' face was lit with God's glory, revealing where he had been and who was speaking to him (Exodus 34:29; 2 Corinthians 3:7). Moses' face was radiant because he'd climbed the mountain and spent time with God. His face reflected God's presence and transforming power.

As you trust God for climbing faith, your life will tell your own God-empowered story. Then like Moses, when others see you, a workmanship of Him, your face will bring courage to those parents who feel weak and frail, and whose hopes have worn thin.

Unlike Moses, your radiance won't be short-lived. Jesus is your Savior, Lord, and friend. He is Father God's glorious brightness, and the express image of His person. He upholds all things by the word of His power. He Himself has purged your sins. He sat down on the right hand of the Majesty on high. He has given you faith as the fruit of the Holy Spirit. Your brightness, your radiance, reflects His glory in the faith climb (Hebrews 1:3).

The view that faith's height unfolds renders to your heart love's brilliance, like sun glistening on gold (2 Corinthians 4:6).

Gear up! God is with you.

THE ANTIDOTE OF FAITH

Faith, though it may feel like it is slipping from time to time, isn't easily diminished or lost; instead, it takes God at His word and lets time have its way. It is the antidote to stress—not just to manage it, but also to rescue you out of its suffocating, toxic effects. Faith detoxes your brain, leaving it free to experience restful peace.

Seem impossible? That's okay. Again, it's not about you working hard to remain in faith. Faith does the work for you.

You are increasing. Faith is lifting you. Faith is transforming your thinking and therefore your wisdom. Creative applications are evolving. It's becoming clearer why the Bible speaks of faith with such urgency. "Have faith in God" (Mark 11:22; Acts 20:21; 27:25; Romans 5:1; 1 Peter 1:21). It's God's invitation into a substantial increase. Apostle Paul's words echo Christ's: "And now, dear brother and sisters, one final thing. Fix your thoughts on what is true, and honorable, and right, and pure, and lovely, and admirable. Think about things that are excellent and worthy of praise" (Philippians 4:8 NLT).

The Holy Spirit will enable you to fix your thoughts on these "things" Paul refers to in Philippians 4:8. You literally will "put on the mind of Christ" and "clothe yourself in the Lord Jesus" by "letting the peace of Christ rule in your heart" (Romans 13:14; Colossians 3:15).

Tell Me Again, Lord, Please

Tell me again, Lord, what You will do.
Tell me again, Lord, how to love you.
Tell me again, Lord, about glorified living.
Tell me again, Lord, about merciful giving.
Bring back to my mind what it means to have faith.
Encourage my heart as I patiently wait.

You belong to a loving, eternal family. You are among His chosen. He delights in you. And, yes, you are in process. You are transitioning, learning, and transforming. Your faith matures as you process through each new challenge. It rises alongside your skill level and parenting wisdom.

When you go to your bed at the end of a long day, when does real rest begin to take place? When your legs are hanging over the side? When you are sitting up with your back leaning on the wall or headboard? When you fall asleep in that halfway sitting up position, you are ready at a moment's notice for the next crisis, but it's not good rest. True rest takes place in your bed when you can throw all your weight on it.

PRAY

Father God, I believe; help my unbelief. Help me understand that faith has already been granted me. When I don't feel faith, I choose to believe Your words that clearly state that You have given faith to me as a deposit of Your grace. I may not be able to see just yet how I can make it, but I do believe You have called me up the mountain. I choose to faith climb. I choose to believe that I can trust You all the way to the top. I choose to believe You will give me the skill to trust the tools, one step at a time, as I climb. One day I will feel safe again. You will be with me, and my life will reveal Your glory. All because of Jesus and the merciful gift of the Holy Spirit, I am gaining the peace that passes understanding. Thank you for keeping me from falling.

REFLECT

1. What have you experienced that will be a comfort or practical aid to another parent who hasn't yet seen the extravagant view from the top?

2. Which one of the thought fixes would be a good choice for you to practice today: true, honorable, right, pure, lovely, or admirable?

7

Elephant Sense: Where Do I Look?

Moving from drained, emotionless, and apathetic to watered, grounded, and renewed

YOU HAVE THE brain and desire to work the problem, but sometimes the pieces don't seem to come together to make the picture complete. Maybe you've asked all the questions you know to ask. You've searched and researched, but your questions remain. Surface answers are not as deep as the need. Where to next?

When Gail reaches this place, she says she could actually feel an empty space growing within. "It felt dry and like something was dying inside." She couldn't put her finger on the problem. Well-meaning, caring friends offered her a dinner out, but her enjoyment of time with them had no appeal. "I didn't want to be impolite. I just wasn't interested. I was in an emotional drought. Something had drained every ounce of my desire for relational interaction. It was like being thirsty and yet not sure where to locate replenishing, clear, cool water."

Be assured, water is ahead for you. And just as this time is real now, so is the time to come when you arrive at a healthy, healing, transformative place.

Whatever "empty place" you find yourself in is part of your journey. You are moving forward. Be certain—water is coming.

Proverbs 25:25 says, "Like cold water to a weary soul is good news from a distant land." Galatians 6:9 says, "Let us not become weary in doing good, for at the proper time we will reap a harvest if we do not give up."

WORDS THAT HEAL

Have you ever had that awkward experience when you were clueless as to how to approach someone that has suffered terribly or is still suffering from a tragic loss? That's how it was for Christen and Jeffrey when they first met Jack and Kayle.

Jack and Kayle were invited to attend a luncheon for parents with children of special needs. They considered and accepted, not because they fit that criterion but because they too had faced a drastic change in circumstances from a tragedy that impacted their lives forever. Their child had become a victim, leading to death. It had caused them to feel like they were buried alive underground.

Jack seemed to reach the surface sooner than Kayle. She remained in an inner state of extreme drought. It took years before she could begin to speak about it and then only barely. The group could possibly be another step forward for them both.

Jack and Kayle introduced themselves to the group. They began softly and calmly sharing a portion of their personal story. As the details were revealed, all of the parents seemed to be holding their breath. They were stunned into silence!

How could anyone recover after suffering that kind of tragedy? No one had an answer, not that they would have said it out loud even if they had a comforting thought or practical advice out of respect for the couple's painful loss. Only God could revive such ravaged souls. His merciful, all-powerful, miraculous resurrection life was their only hope.

Immediately after Jack and Kayle shared their heart-felt struggles, the waiters came into the room to serve dessert. No sounds of friendly, reflective chatter could be heard. Instead, a man at one table could be heard softly telling his story with tears flowing down his face. Two women at another table with heads bowed were holding hands. The waiters slowly, quietly moved through the crowd, whispering their choices as the rest of the parents sat in utter silence.

Christen tentatively approached Kayle. "I'm so stunned that you are able to speak and share with us here today."

"I couldn't do it for a long time," replied Kayle. "I was no more than an outward shell. I had completely lost my way. I not only didn't know where to look, but I no longer even wanted to look for answers. After a while when people came to visit, showing their love and trying to encourage me, I would sit and listen patiently. But it was as if nothingness merged into nothingness. Blank. Empty. No love, no voice of encouragement penetrated."

Even though both Jack and Kayle were devoted followers of Jesus before the terrible tragedy struck, no Scripture or biblical promise had seemed to make any difference. Life as they knew it was over. They felt dead on the inside.

"Then one day a friend came to visit," Kayle continued. "I sat dutifully listening as I always had, pretending I was a person that could hear and receive. Somewhere in the mesh of words, the visitor quoted a Scripture passage from the book of Job. 'At least there is hope for a tree: If it is cut down, it will sprout again, and its new shoots will not fail. Its roots may grow old in the ground and its stump die in the soil, yet at the scent of water it will bud and put forth shoots like a plant. But a man dies and is laid low; he breathes his last and is no more' (Job 14:7–10).

"From that moment on, I began to heal. It was not from the scent of water, but just from hearing about the scent of water from the Word of God that life began to form a tiny sprout from inside the dead stump of a tree."

As Kayle spoke, Christen sensed she was on sacred ground. She went to her Bible and read the Scripture for herself. Why, out of all the wonderful promises in the Bible, would this odd Scripture speak so gloriously to Kayle's inward being? Why would it cause resurrection life to activate the journey toward restoration for her and her husband? To Christen, it just didn't make sense. It was a mystery.

Sometimes mystery. Sometimes not. Sometimes no words from others can help. Only He knows how to resurrect, restore, and heal. What He uses can often be a complete conundrum.

CONUNDRUMS

Remember Gideon's lament. He couldn't believe God would come to the rescue. And, even if He did, Gideon was positive God couldn't use him to protect him and his family from the incoming danger.

Job tells his personal story of restoration after devastating family losses. In Job 10:12 he says, "You gave me life and showed me kindness, and in your providence watched over my spirit." The King James Version says it this way: "Thou has granted me life and favour, and thy visitation hath preserved my spirit." In both versions we can see that after losing absolutely everything, beyond a shadow of a doubt, Job knew that only God could have rescued his spirit to live again.

Hezekiah, another biblical leader, had a story that rang out with the same tone. In Isaiah 38:16, he marveled at God's power to bring life out of overwhelming challenges. "Lord, by such things people live; and my spirit finds life in them too. You restored me to health and let me live."

Full comprehension of how God actually works His restoration miracles may remain a mystery. The fact is that He does bring hope for today. John 6:63 gives a hint of that truth in Jesus' discourse with His upset disciples when He explains, "The Spirit gives life; the flesh counts for nothing. The words I have spoken to you—they are full of the Spirit and life."

No matter what surprising way God intervenes, when His Spirit initiates intervention, it brings life. We can look to God's Spirit, the Comforter, for supernatural provision when nothing, absolutely nothing is going to bring joy out of sorrow, hope out of pain, grace out of despair, rest out of severe exhaustion, and peace for the depleted soul. Whether He sends a dream, memory, or angelic visitation; a voice here or a touch there; or even the sound of wind or the scent of water, help is coming. It can appear in starling ways.

He is going to provide a supernatural ability to sense His presence as you wait for Him and continue to look to Him. Give it time. He knows your needs.

Counselor Angela Timmons has a passion for studying the behavioral science of elephants. She shares her thoughts about the correlation of our lives and elephants in this story.

Coded for Life by the Master Creator

It appeared that Mama had been separated from the herd. Was she sick? Had she been injured? The tires of the tour van gripped the uneven dirt of the warn path, and the van rocked and squeaked as it crept cautiously and silently closer toward this mammoth of a specimen. With cameras and binoculars in place, we pondered reasons why she was so far behind the pack. Finally it was evident. There, between her thunderous yet graceful movements, was a newborn. The tour guide, so proficient and knowledgeable, estimated the calf to be about twenty-four hours old.

The clumsy, unsteady newborn was learning already how to negotiate the landscape. It was fragile, its movement unsure. Mama, the protector, was very methodical and majestic in instinctively monitoring the tiny tot. She was being watchful for predators yet encouraging the calf with her trunk; she was showing, guiding, waiting, and signaling in elephant language that could be understood by not just her kind but by all who watched. It seemingly was too much for the little one to grasp. Yet, instinctively, Mama was transferring to this newborn the wisdom that one day would be required for it to sustain, defend, protect, and survive on its own—to be as majestic and capable as its mother.

Elephants are a fascinating study. They are incredibly instinctive, intelligent, and ferociously protective. These huge land mammals have exceptional and amazingly interesting traits. Whether Asian or African, these creatures exhibit a family system that advanced intelligence is obliged to replicate. They have highly developed social systems. The complex folds in their brain allow these largest of living herbivorous land mammals to experience emotion and social awareness. They experience compassion for the weak, display grief over companion loss, and show great care and concern for others of their kind. Their advanced understanding gives them, through the use of their senses, a greater ability to navigate the social and emotional. It also gives them the ability to acquire life-sustaining food and water for day-to-day survival.

Just as with the elephant, the greatness of our Master Creator has coded within our DNA a structure or model process for life, including the instincts for family. With the Holy Spirit, we have the ability to be the most effective in our daily challenges. We have the ability to sense the scent that will help us sustain and endure. Our coding, when connected with a sustaining power source greater than ourselves, provides protection and instincts for navigating the dusty, uneven, and irregular roads of life. We are privileged to have been given special senses and abilities too, which allow the discovery of "living water."

Each of us, like the elephant protecting and providing for its young, has the spiritual instinct to protect, guard, and nurture. God provides what we need to survive through the Bible, the life-giving, sustaining, therapeutic living water necessary to heal, restore, rebuild, and renew us through life's journey.

ELEPHANTS AND THE SCENT OF WATER

Scents and sounds can have life-giving, significant purpose. What seems impossible or insignificant can become an answer. Learning about how God has equipped His creatures for their survival inspires a renewed strength to trust that He has provision for you as well.

An elephant needs immense amounts of water. It can consume 40–60 gallons of water a day. How then can this animal be expected to survive in a land where dry seasons and drought are more common than not? And yet it does.

The answer lies in divine design. Elephants are well equipped for survival through their amazing abilities to find water. In times of drought, they know to migrate. If a drought is severe, they migrate far away, to other areas where water is more plentiful. They also know to dig into dry streambeds or other spots to uncover water that is not visible on the surface. They use their feet, trunks, and tusks to pound the ground and dig until an adequate supply of water appears. The amusing sight of elephants circling, stomping, and digging together has been described as their dance for water.

Elephants' ability to pick up the scent of water saves their lives. God has given them unique abilities to search for water and migrate to wet areas where they are safe to enjoy the water of life they cannot live without. Some reports indicate elephants' sense of smell is so keen that it enables them to locate life-giving water a distance of twelve miles or more away. They wave their trunks in the air, gathering scent particles that give them not only the smell of water but also the distance and direction to go to find it. Their trunks detect potential dangers, helping them decide between bodies of water when they pick up the scent of more than one potential source.

Their abilities sound similar to what King David says about surviving and searching for God's help in Psalm 63:1–8.

> You, God, are my God, earnestly I seek you; I thirst for you, my whole being longs for you, in a dry and parched land where there is no water. I have seen you in the sanctuary and beheld your power and your glory. Because your love is better than life, my lips will glorify you. I will praise you as long as I live, and in your name I will lift up my hands. I will be fully satisfied as with the richest of foods; with singing lips my mouth will praise you. On my bed I remember you; I think of you through the watches of the night. Because you are my help, I sing in the shadow of your wings. I cling to you; your right hand upholds me.

In an interview with Denette and her sister, Carole, Denette said about her son dealing with muscular degeneration, "Bill is a living example to me every day. He is more often accepting and resilient, while I find myself getting so frustrated at times."

"I agree," Carole added. "Children don't seem to carry the emotional baggage that we adults do from our experiences."

"So true," Denette replied. "Bill is usually accepting and resilient, and yet there were times he just refused to budge from what he wanted."

Nancy Miller's four stages that parents of children with special needs go through—*surviving, searching, settling,* and *separating*—are not linear. Often the emotions of several can be experienced at the same time, as evidenced by what Denette shares here. For her, the *settling* stage included letting go but not giving up.

A Change of Place

We had no choice. It was time to move our son, Bill, into assisted living. It was the best we could do for him, at least temporarily.

When we told him the news, he became unusually argumentative. "You can't force me! I won't do it!" I felt like my life was hanging by a thread. I knew it would take the grace of God to get him to want to go, but Bill absolutely refused. I didn't know where to begin to look for help.

I found one place I thought could work. It was homey and lovely with a garden and a dog. But when I took him there, he wouldn't even get out of the car to look, yelling at me, "No, I won't go!" I knew I had to do this, but it was killing me inside. Every fiber in my being said this wasn't supposed to be this way. When God allowed me to adopt Bill, I prayed and vowed that as long as I was alive, I would take care of him. I always figured we would die together, which I realize now was very foolish and naïve.

I didn't know what to do. I prayed. My family was praying. My friends were praying. And then one day I saw a sign in a grocery store of a new assisted living place. It was so beautiful, but I just knew I couldn't afford it. When I went to check it out, it was so lovely I was ready to move in myself. It had just opened, no waiting list. Excited, I found out the place would take Medicare, and so I made a plan to show Bill.

"Bill, you need to understand. It's not *if* you want to live in assisted living, but it is *which one* are you going to live in." That was how I prepared him for what was about to happen.

We drove to the place. To my amazement, Bill said, "Oh, wow, look at this." What a relief. It wasn't but a few days, and he was moved in. He loved it. Once he settled in, he began making friends. He actually ran for an election to be VP of the residency at thirty-eight years old. Mr. Social, Bill, was a happy-go-lucky fellow, enjoying the other residents.

When I didn't know where to look, I kept crying out to God for help. Who knew a simple grocery store bulletin board would offer such a tremendous gift? Only God could have directed me to such a find!

Over and over again help came from unexpected sources. After he moved in, I told Bill he had to walk regularly to keep his legs strong. When my urging turned into a fight, I told him it was his body and his choice and stopped arguing with him. Again, I turned the matter over to God in prayer.

A neighbor in the residency was in a wheelchair due to a stroke. He had workout equipment in his room. One day we were chatting, playing a board game, when this resident commented, "I work out every day." Later I mentioned to Bill, "I think he would enjoy having someone to work out with. What do you think?" In no time, both of them were working out together. What a huge blessing to have them help each other. They loved it, and they both got stronger. All that I had to go through with Bill made really good sense.

Each time we didn't have a clue, the answer would come from an unexpected source, something that wasn't obvious on the surface in the moment. Looking back, it seems like help would come and we had no idea how in the world it could have happened. Each time we were stunned, relieved, scratched our heads, and turn to our heavenly Father with deep gratefulness to say, "Thank you, thank you, thank you."

Denette discovered that, like the elephants' sense, the resources needed at every stage can be divine and can come from the most amazing places.

SHIFTING PERSPECTIVES

Dr. Rev. Laurie A. Vervaecke, LCPC, LCCC, is a licensed clinical pastoral counselor, licensed clinical Christian counselor, speaker, and president of Utah Childhelp. Her thoughts are an expert's perspective on shifting ideas, which enables a fusion of wisdom for your daily decision making.

> When you think of the word *shift* as a verb, it means to put something aside or replace it by another. A shift transfers a person from one place or position to another much like a car shifts gears from one ratio or arrangement to another. When you apply a shift to a sport like baseball, it could mean a repositioning strategy or change.
>
> A shift is also a modifier key on a keyboard, which with a gentle, simple action, alters the output. A shift key affects other keys on a keyboard just like your perspective shifts affect the other people in your life. On the keyboard, the key changes the normal lowercase letter to an uppercase letter. In a similar way, you are pressing into key elements of change while you are balancing your "new normal" perspectives. As you are willing to shift your perspectives on occasion, you will experience a heightened response, a different expression of normal that builds clearer communication and a finer touch to your day.

Shifting perspectives include being realistic about what may happen and accepting it, as Denette's story reveals. "The situations you face as you move forward with your child's changing needs can throw you into a perspective check," said Denette. "For me, I had to ask myself what was most important. If my son died two years earlier because he didn't walk, would the loss be greater than ten years of arguing, stress, and a ruined relationship with him? My answer was no, it wasn't worth it. My perspective changed. My motives remained the same—to do the best for my son as I could for the rest of my life. Defining what was best changed. And my perspectives on what was important and why it was important have continued to morph throughout the years."

Later in the interview with Denette, her sister, Carole, reflected healing to Denette. "What he needed back then, you gave him. What he needs today, you are giving him. You pushed him when it was necessary. Today is different. Your role, your function, shifts. How you see yourself as a person and as a mom in your relationship with him shifts too. You are a good person, leaning on the goodness of God, trusting for the best outcome possible."

"Yes," Denette replied, "that is true with any child growing into adulthood. Relationship, perspective, and interactions shift with time. Mine had to morph from what I wanted for Bill to be and do as his mother to what was more realistic and sometimes what he was willing to do."

FAITH IS A VERB

Mary Sue, struggling with the required changes in her and her son's interactions, was exasperated, lost, and at her wit's end, as she would put it. Laying her head down on her desk, numb, an old song came to mind from Sonny and Cher. Over and over in her mind she could hear them sing some of those unforgettable lines ("I've got you to understand") and the chorus ("I got you babe, I got you babe").

As she remembered the lyrics, there came an unexplainable lifting. She whispered, "You're amazing, God. You use anything and everything to get your point across. Thank you." She stood up from the desk and walked out the door, once again encouraged that what seemed like a dead end just a few minutes ago was now surrendered into His care.

When we place faith in Christ Jesus, it becomes the faith of Christ Himself. In many languages, *faith* is a verb, an action verb. What we do, how we act, demonstrates what we believe. Hope, the companion of faith, reminds us that one day the pain or struggles we face will not define us. He turns second guesses into second chances as we look to Him. Facing our life challenges is not about having faith for something as much as it is having the faith of Someone, our heavenly Father, His Son and our Lord Jesus Christ, and the guiding, comforting abiding Holy Spirit.

LIVING WATER IS A SPIRITUAL DYNAMIC

A *dynamic* is a force that stimulates change or progress. Jesus referred to Himself as living water, or water that is fresh and flows from God's provision as a dynamic for change. The book of John records a story of a Samaritan woman who came alone to a nearby well where Jesus was resting. As she approaches, Jesus asks her to give Him a drink. She is shocked. In those days, men didn't openly speak to strange women, and Jews avoided speaking to Samaritans.

"How come you, a Jew, are asking me, a Samaritan woman, for a drink?" she questions. Jesus answers, "If you knew the generosity of God, and who I am, you would be asking *me* for a drink, and I would give you fresh, living water." He continues His discourse with the woman. "Everyone who drinks this water will get thirsty again and again. Anyone who drinks the water I give will never thirst—not ever. The water I give will be an artesian spring within, gushing fountains of endless life." (John 4:7–15 MSG)

Everyone needs living water. It doesn't matter if you feel like life has cut you down at the core or you're an old, dead stump, lying dormant. Your spirit is on the search.

When you are born of God's Spirit, the spirit within you is eternal. You may not know where to look for what you need, but your spirit will pick up the scent of water by the help of the Spirit of God. As it is with the wind that blows wherever it pleases and its source is not obvious, you may not be able to tell where the scent is coming from or where it is leading, but you will know its presence.

The nature of the elephant causes it to smell the water particles in the air, and it begins its dance for water. The nature of the Spirit of God within your spirit will lead you to His living water. Your soul will dance again!

Wind Patterns

Who could knit the wind or pearl it into place?
Only God its author could turn this skein into lace!
Even so you go
As the Holy Spirit bids you will
And as oft as He prompts His profiting
The design is changing still.
Until He gathers His elect
From the earth's farthest ends,
He knits and pearls your blessings
Like He patterns out the winds.

He Is Jesus

Intimate moments one by one
Build a lifelong bond with the Holy One.
His tender heart is waiting
To reveal His loving Son.
And to whom shall He make known His will?
To each willing soul that longs to be won.

This is life
This is beauty
He is Jesus
Not just duty
Not dry or boring
But sweet and knowing
Oh how His presence sparkles
My heart beholds and marvels.

This is life
This is beauty
He is Jesus
Not just duty
He will lift, compel, and draw
Until we are wrapped in reverent awe!

PRAY

Father God, I trust I am Your workmanship in Christ Jesus and my instincts come from Your Spirit. In time, I believe I will discover the necessary provisions even when they are not obvious at the moment. I believe You, Father, are activating a healthy, life-giving transformation process from whatever stage or "dry empty place" in which I find myself right now. In my journey of transformation, I will continue to trust Your leading. I choose to believe water is ahead. The day will come when my thirst is quenched and my longing soul is renewed. I smile at the thought of my personal elephant dance!

REFLECT

1. "May your choices reflect your hopes, not your fears." —Nelson Mandela
   In what ways have you made choices to remain on the journey of faith when there is no sign of desperately needed provision? How have these choices affected your sense of well-being? Which of them eventually came full circle, enabling you to experience an answer or provision?

2. At the moment an answer or provision came to you, did it seem to be from an unexpected source or seem completely illogical at first? What thoughts about it came to you later?

3. Who do you know who has had a similar, unexpected and dramatic transformation that at first may have seemingly come out of nowhere? How was that person's story encouraging or faith building for you?

8

Buttercups Under Ice: You Call This Progress?

Moving from a tense, snap, sting, ouch to soothing, reliance, comfort, and resilience

WHILE YOU ARE in the settling in stage, it may be helpful to recall the childhood story of the rabbit and the hare. The race is not always won by the swiftest. Rather, victory belongs to the one who remains constant with the smallest increments of progress. It's okay to creep and sometimes crawl on your way to the finish line.

Without a realistic perspective of what it means to *win* the race, you could find yourself opposing what is actual positive progress. For example, some parents wonder if the next aid they provide for their child is a sign they are giving up. The use of a wheelchair or other equipment, for example, is not an act of unbelief or a sign of resignation. Instead, it is a concrete action of settling in for the whole of the journey.

MAINTAINING THE BALANCE

Does your grocery store sell broccoli bunched together with a wide, thick, blue rubber band? Imagine cutting it in half and you and a friend each holding tightly to one end. It's a game. You back up and see who lets go first. Eyes squeezed tight, head tucked, each of you slowly, carefully pulls against the other. Snap! Whoever lets go first loses the battle, but whoever holds tightly to the end "gets it," and it leaves a mark.

Balancing the tension between enjoying the smoother, gentler times and being prepared for the "snap" is a choice that takes practice. The sting of disappointments, especially when they are unexpected, can cancel out the pleasurable, humorous, and momentary delights. Snap!

So how can you find and maintain the balance in positive, life-giving ways? Therapist Faith Raimer shares her ideas.

Going from Snap to Zap

Like holding the plastic covering in place to protect our newspaper on a rainy day, rubber bands are functional in a myriad of ways. How many times in my youth did I scout out a strong one to hold my thick, curly hair in a ponytail or a larger one to hold my stretched out knee socks? Today there are the colorful, sturdy ones grocers use for packaging produce. I especially like the purple, don't you?

It turns out that the snap of a rubber band is sometimes the preferred method of treatment in therapy. It even has a name, The Rubber Band Technique, and has proven to be effective to discourage or eradicate unwanted behaviors. Simply stated, it allows a mental shift to occur that can change a mind-set or help break a habit.

Why is this snap concept important? A well-known quote by Henry Ford, "Whether you think you can or you can't, you're right," is a good reminder of the significance and impact your thoughts can have in your life. Permit me to offer a few over-simplified, non-technical words about feelings, thoughts, and behavior to shed more light on this idea. Your *feelings* are primarily based on your emotions. Your *thoughts* help you mentally evaluate, sort, and label your feelings. Men are especially good at quickly sorting because they are more apt to see things in their mind's eye in black and white—it's this or it's that, period. Most women need more time to gather, unravel, sort, weigh, and justify feelings to come to a "rational" conclusion. Your *behavior* is feeling or thought-driven or a combination of the two.

Humans, like animals, have an automatic system within the brain called the "fight or flight response" that signals us to react immediately when faced with imminent danger. It is a physiological response that triggers a release of hormones to prepare the body to stand firm or flee. Unlike animals, however, humans have the intellectual capacity to acquire and apply knowledge and skills. Under normal conditions, this capacity allows us to consider a situation and offer a reasoned response rather than simply rely on a knee-jerk reaction. Responding with reason and skill requires forethought and practice. Being reactive is automatic and doesn't require much effort.

A *pattern* is a positive action or behavior repeated on a regular basis that is beneficial. A *habit* is a repeated behavior that can be negative and when practiced on a regular basis, can be harmful. Patterns are easily managed, corrected, or changed as appropriate to the individual or situation. For example, Ruth developed a loving pattern of baking sweet treats to offer Sue whenever she came to visit. During one visit, Sue let her know she appreciated the thought but was trying to avoid sugar. Ruth continued offering her loving kindness by shifting from confections to carrots. Sue could munch to her heart's content. Peace was restored, and the problem was solved.

Habits are more challenging and difficult to change. Ron, for example, had a habit of complaining. He seemed to have a knack for casting clouds on blue skies. People grew tired of his negativism and began to shun him. When a brave friend finally confronted Ron about his bad habit, Ron reacted with surprise and anger. He defended his behavior by accusing his friend of being mean-spirited and out of touch with reality. After calming down, Ron considered the truth in what he heard. He realized he was wrong. He could see he needed to change but didn't know where to start. He had been a complainer for so long it seemed natural to grumble and find fault and unnatural not to do so. As part of his therapy, Ron was asked to try using the Rubber Band Technique.

Here is how the technique works. You start by placing a sturdy rubber band that fits comfortably on your wrist. You tell yourself what you want to quit doing, such as making negative statements such as "That guy is such a jerk." The moment the habit you wish to break begins, you take hold of the rubber band, stretch it out, and let it go against your wrist. SNAP! As you feel the stinging snap, you say something positive like, "That guy is doing the best he can." By replacing the negative with positive, you shift your thoughts and retrain your brain. By making this choice of action a repeated pattern, you empower yourself to think and act from your heart instead of your head. You are teaching yourself to make conscious decisions that are responsive instead of reactive.

Much to the delight of Ron and his friends, this technique worked for him. It can work for you too. If you are in the habit of putting yourself down, for example, you can replace the negative self-talk with words that are encouraging and uplifting. Using the Rubber Band Technique, you ZAP a bad habit, like saying "I'm a failure," and replace it with a pattern that says "I am capable and competent." Even if you don't believe it to begin with, you will soon be able to see the truth in it for yourself.

Most of us, if we are honest with ourselves, could use some help dealing with our habits and unwanted or reactive behavior. Consider adding a simple rubber band to your tools-for-life kit. The investment is minor. The rewards are major. What color is your band?

IN THE WAITING TIME

Whatever's happening in this hour, your practical reality will usually take precedence over what you think the future can bring. At the same time, the renewed mind is always adjusting perspectives to be ready for what is ahead. Therapist Carmenza Herrera Mendez, shares her thoughts on waiting time.

> There are times when parents must continue to practice drills, or attempts, to get a behavior or interaction going with a child through seemingly endless trials and errors. These drills may cover everything from a game or a self-help skill (bathing) to trying to get a child to try new food to how to respond in a life/death situation. To the naked eye, it may seem like nothing is happening, no progress is being made.
>
> This place, seemingly without progress, is actually a time of waiting in the sense that there isn't discernable change. It is the time I believe it is important to remind parents that they must be clear on the information they have from their specialized team of doctors or therapists concerning the goals and realistic expectations they are working toward.

Sometimes unhealthy tension is increased when your personal bar has been set too high for physical or emotional changes in your child at a given point in time. The higher the bar, the greater the distance down. You may sense a need to define and redefine expectations and time elements for the changes you wish to come to pass. When goals are set too high or too soon, the inevitable disappointment can be a forerunner to depression. Bitterness, anger, and frustration can set in. Before you know it, you can find yourself immersed in harmful resentment toward others, especially authority figures who pointed you toward another medication or use of a particular piece of equipment.

Susan and Kevin were convinced that everything that happened was either from God or from the devil. There was no in between. They saw no discernable progress as a step backward. They despised the day as a failure. They saw themselves in daily warfare. When asked about the latest effort to bring about change or growth, you could hear the anguish in their voice: "The devil won this one." It was yet another test between good and evil, success and failure. Sadly, they spent years in this mind-set. They felt like they were losing if they let go of their desperate hatred of the current progress in lieu of finding a place for tomorrow's potential. There never seemed to be a day for celebrating the sweet moments, treasure hunting for gratefulness, or rest from the battle to give them a chance to uncover a pebble of joy.

One day Connie was sinking in the mire of disappointment. With a deep sigh, she journaled these prayerful words.

Very Still, Very Small

In my mind's eye, I can see a candle is burning low. A light breeze is blowing gently through the darkened window. I can see myself getting up to blow out the flickering candle, what seems to be my only light.

Jesus, is this a message from You? Lord Jesus, is this You encouraging me to rise up, greet the breeze, and blow out the candle? Am I to believe there will be an upcoming noonday sun of answers from this tiny glint, very small breeze, and still morn? Even though this is all I see and feel, do You want me to have hope and trust in Your loving provision for me?

Then, a soft, comforting answer seemed to emerge with a simple reply, "Yes." Instantly, I could feel a strengthening resolve and the tension lifting.

At the same time, words from the Bible came to mind. Psalm 37:4–6, "Take delight in the Lord, and he will give you the desires of your heart. Commit your way to the Lord; trust in him and he will do this: He will make your righteous reward shine like the dawn, your vindication like the noonday sun."

Sandra was recovering from the devastating loss of her husband and a mountain of debt. She shared the basis of her learning curve with a simple phrase, "Nurture hope and faith will grow." Each incremental step in her progress came as a result of significant effort alongside great provision from her Lord. It wasn't easy. It took perseverance and resilience, and yet she said she could not deny God's provision along the way. Today she continues to celebrate her discoveries of His equipping presence that transported her through it all.

Advanced preparation for "no matter what" is not a negative evaluation for your child's future potential. Nor is it any kind of displeasing unbelief in what God can do. It's not about giving up. Your wait time is about trusting—trusting "no matter what!"

2 Corinthians 12:9 says, "But he said to me, 'My grace is sufficient for you, for my power is made perfect in weakness.' Therefore I will boast all the more gladly about my weaknesses, so that Christ's power may rest on me." Philippians 4:13 says, "I can do all this through him who gives me strength."

THE DAY OF SMALL THINGS

In Zechariah 4:10, an angel asks Zerubbabel a question: "Who dares despise the day of small things?" If you despise something, you loath, scorn, look down on, or hate it. Strong words. Strong feelings. The absence of measurable or recognized progress can evoke a negative response. It has the potential of becoming all-consuming to the point of obliterating any sense of true progress. You can be left with strong feelings of hatred that become like darts aimed directly at anyone who hints you should back off a bit.

Woe to the person who dares to tell you the progress "thus far" is good enough for now. You don't want to hear it. This rejection can prevent feelings of thankfulness and the hope that comes with even the smallest increments of progress. In short, you miss out on the celebration of small things.

In the story of Zechariah, I can imagine the mockers taunting the Israelites for their slow, incremental progress. They saw their weakness, poverty, and the fact that no one befriended them or their cause as pitiful. These mockers despised them, taunting them with words like "What will these feeble people do? Will they build?" (4:10). They saw them as fools for even trying because they appeared impotent. But the point of the angel's question, "Who dares despise the day of small things?" was to point out the absurdity of the mockers. With God on their side, they were unstoppable!

Each day is an opportunity for you to consider what small thing can be accomplished in it. Recognizing what is reasonable for today and what may not be until another day is not in opposition to remaining hopeful and believing for God's best.

Therapist Faith Raimer offers her perspective on small things. "I remember a time when I was coaching a basketball team. I wasn't so much a therapist as I was a mom and a coach. One of the players was Johnny, red haired and freckled, timid and frightened to do anything. He didn't give up and neither did I. One day I encouraged and coached him. I told the kids to pass the ball to Johnny, and they did. We were so shocked when he made a basket. Meanwhile his dad, who finally had come to a game, was outside vomiting because he was drunk. Johnny didn't have the rejoicing of his father, but he had everyone else's."

Denette articulates the difference between giving up and letting go during the settling stage. "Sometimes when I give up or let go, I'm the only person who knows the difference. The big difference between the two choices is inside. When I just give up, I feel hopeless, disgruntled, or maybe even furious. When I let go, I feel grace and peace. On the outside it may look like the same action, but on the inside it's significantly different." When Denette found the grace to let go of what she needed to do relative to her son's future, she felt both more patient and more empowered.

Rather than despising small things why not admire them? Six-year-old Ellen loved putting her coat on without help despite the fact that her little arms shook so wildly she could hardly get them in the sleeves. Aware of her circumstances, her teacher knew to be patient and wait. When Ellen finally succeeded, her big smile and bright eyes were a joy to behold and well worth the wait.

Ellen's teacher admired her courage and persistence. She wondered, if she were in Ellen's place, whether she would have the same amount of determination. Ellen's actions added brightness to her teacher's days. One day as she stood watching Ellen, she could hear the birds harmonizing outside the window, as if they too were admiring little Ellen and singing her praises.

When you redefine what is most important for your child to accomplish at any point in the progress forward, you can better enjoy each precious moment. After all, parenting isn't a sprint—it's a life marathon. As you gain understanding for what is needed for the long run, you will be empowered with a greater degree of patience for today.

Whenever you feel the tension of expectations, it's helpful to ask yourself, Where did this expectation come from?

Is it from my own personal value system?
Is it from the culture at large?
Is it how my family responds?
Is it based on the way people treat us?
Is it all of the above?

Once you determine the source of an expectation, ask yourself whether or not it is healthy. When that question is answered, you can have more satisfaction and personal peace, knowing the difference between what is an unrealistic expectation and what is true for you and your family now.

James Dobson comments in his book, *When God Doesn't Make Sense*, "Paul's secret of contentment emerges from a universal principle of human nature. It is to trust God regardless of the circumstances and not to expect too much perfection in this life. A better day is coming for those whose source of contentment is the personhood of Christ Jesus!"

If

(patterned after Rudyard Kipling's poem "If—")

If you can keep your head
when all about you are losing theirs and blaming it on you;
If you can trust yourself
when all men doubt you but make allowance for their doubting too;

If you can wait and not be tired by waiting
or being lied about, don't deal in lies
or being hated, don't give way to hating
or try to look good in other people's eyes;

If you can dream and not make dreams your master;
If you can think and not make thoughts your aim;
If you can meet with triumph and disaster
and treat those two impostors just the same;

If you can be content when you find yourself abased
and keep your joy as others about you abound
and be at peace with the gain that godliness brings
and its strength to turn your life around;

If you can bear to hear the truth you've spoken
twisted by knaves to make a trap for fools
or watch the lives of others about you be broken
yet remain ready to build them up with God-given tools;

If you can make one heap of all your earnings
and give them away at heaven's request
and start again with faith as your only beginning
and never breathe a word, content in God's rest;

If you can force your heart and nerve and sinew
to serve your turn long after others are gone
and so hold on when there is nothing in you
except God's will that says to them, "Hold on!";

If you can talk with crowds and keep your virtue
or walk with kings but not lose the common touch;
If neither foes nor loving friends can hurt you
or if all men count with you, but none too much;

If you can fill the unforgiving minute
with sixty seconds worth of mercy's distance run;
Yours is the earth and everything that's in it
and, what's infinitely more, you'll be God's miracle of love.

Your heavenly Father offers you a continual flow of loving acceptance and understanding to wash away your disappointments today and replace them with His admiration for you for even the smallest efforts.

People may mock you or think you are foolish for finding treasure in the beauty you have discovered along the way. It happens. They just don't understand your secret and haven't learned themselves the joy of treasure hunting for even the smallest valuable pebble of life. But God does. He is on your side, cheering you on every step of the way.

Encourage your heart with His truth. Build strength, courage, and endurance in your soul with Scriptures such as Romans 4:18, "Against all hope, Abraham in hope believed and so became the father of many nations," and Mark 9:23, "'If you can?' said Jesus. 'Everything is possible for him who believes.'" And if your spirit continues to sink like a rock in the pond, consider praying the same prayer the doubting father in the Mark 9:24 prayed, "I do believe; help me overcome my unbelief!"

Make a quality choice to let your heart be immersed in a relationship with your Creator, almighty God, and His Son Jesus Christ. Believe that God will provide the strengthening resilience needed for your soul and the spirit needed for the reports, medical professionals, insurance companies, schools, or organizations that seem only to affirm that nothing can change for the better. Resilience is the ability to recover again from stress, drastic change, or loss. It brings flexibility and is the opposite of rigidity. Even if the negative reports end up being true, you can and will be equipped to handle them. You will do more than survive. With God on your side, you will thrive in His care and unconditional love.

Your heavenly Father will quiet your soul and spark your spirit to sing. When He does, you will be better able to handle the tension between negative and positive expectations. And you will be amazed at your acquired growth in strength of character that helps smooth the stony path of challenges confronting you every day. Your sun-bright, yellow blossoms will become visible under life's thick layer of ice. The days are coming when you will be surprised to hear yourself just humming along.

Wait

It is in silence you can hear the smallest sound.
As my soul waits upon the Lord,
His fruitfulness will abound.

1 John 3:1-3 says, "See what great love the Father has lavished on us, that we should be called children of God! And that is what we are! The reason the world does not know us is that it did not know him. Dear friends, now we are children of God, and what we will be has not yet been made known. But we know that when Christ appears, we shall be like him, for we shall see him as he is. All who have this hope in him purify themselves, just as he is pure."

Buttercups Under Ice

"How foolish!" some would say.
"You're always hoping tomorrow for what didn't happen today."
Always? Yes.
Foolish? I don't think so.
After all, why not believe it will happen on the morrow?

Only fear holds back trusting once more.
Consider the peaceful spirit hope has in store.

You may feel as if you won't be able to bear the pain
if you find your hopes were embraced in vain.
Just remember life extends beyond this hour.
Trust God's loving care and willingness to empower.

For those who have eyes to see, nature tells a hopeful tale.
Consider creation and the many lessons we can learn
from the flower, butterfly, or silkworm.
And what is her good news?
There's reason for hope beyond each dark veil.

You've seen the photographs. I have too.
Remarkable, what a wonder, wow!
What seems impossible is true!

One marvel caught in a photographer's lens
was buttercups blooming under ice—
a captured phenomenon of life.
If the picture had not immortalized it,
who would have believed it could be so?

No one would guess that buttercups could grow
not only in the severest cold,
but bloom from beneath ice, surrounded by snow.

My heart leaps in affirmation.
It's true, God's mercies are sure.
I stand, awed in admiration.

Hope, like a winter bridegroom, expectantly lifts the veil of obscurity,
revealing God's commitment to you,
which goes beyond the moment into eternity.

Most assuredly there are seasons in life
when you will want to remember those buttercups under ice.
When you're overwhelmed, and tears rush down your face,
don't forget the buttercups emerging from beneath the thick, icy lace.

Scripture warns that hope deferred makes the heart feel sick.
Don't be afraid. Buttercups can bloom where you cannot see.
Heaven's voice within will encourage you when hope seems thin.

Buttercups under the ice are nature's reminders
that your earnest expectations,
as yet concealed,
may at any given moment be revealed.
And if by chance your blossoms never come into full view,
still lean on Father God. He will strengthen you.

Until the last night is done, the last breath taken,
hope will endure long, resting in God's salvation.
How about you? Do you believe His Word is true?

PRAY

Heavenly Father, I choose today to step out of any negative evaluations that rob me of seeing from Your perspective. I come out of agreement with the self-thoughts that have held me captive, and I come into agreement with the healthy patience and peace You have stored up for my family. I believe Your love is being lavished upon us. The things we have not yet seen have potential to be revealed in Your timing. Any hopes that do not come to fruition will not alter my abiding trust because I am Your workmanship in Christ Jesus. My family rests in knowing that when You appear, we will be like You. This truth will continue to be our purifying hope. What a glorious day that will be! In the meantime, I choose to hunt for the hidden treasures and the small things. I believe I will see the buttercups under ice.

REFLECT

1. What expectations do you have today? To what extent are they realistic as far as you can tell in your implementation journey?

2. Is it time to add or decrease the level of a particular expectation? If so, to what?

3. How often do you find yourself able to recognize and enjoy even the small things? What one can you think in particular right now?

9

Lion-Hearted Waiting: Can You Hear Me Roar?

Moving from defeat, intimidation, and fainthearted responses to overcoming, courageous, and perseverant reactions

WILTING OR "FAINTING" each time you hear bad news is no longer your first reaction. Okay, maybe you're still working toward it, but you're getting better. News of yet another challenge is not going to convince or even tempt you to give up. No matter how many times you have to go through a struggle or a repeated situation, you are discovering God-given tenacity to persevere.

How can you declare such a wild confidence? You are not only moving through the emotional and practical stages of special needs parenting, but you are also transitioning into a deeper maturity as a believer and follower of Jesus. You are, or soon will be, coming to the settled truth that no matter what the future holds, even if it is less than what you once hoped, you know God is good, you are His child, and He is with you. It is your stake in the ground, your confidence to prevail. Your hope is strengthening your convictions, reinforcing your internal and external strength.

Psalm 31:24 says, "Be strong and take heart, all you who hope in the LORD."

It's likely you no longer think of yourself as a victim. You have begun to experience times when the provision of John 14:27 is prevailing: "Peace I leave with you; my peace I give you. I do not give to you as the world gives. Do not let your heart be troubled and do not be afraid." Courage is growing, even if it seems ever so slowly at times.

THE COURAGE TO CHALLENGE

Christians sometimes vacillate between when it is time to just let something roll on by without much opposition and when to challenge a decision or diagnosis. Jana's story about Jason underscores how courage grows in the face of challenges.

> **Jason, Jana, and the Powers That Be (part 1)**
>
> Once Jason was able to come home from the hospital after his traumatic birth, the diagnosis was even more dreadful: Genetic Abnormality of 1Q.
>
> The doctors said there had been only a couple of cases with this genetic component, and the children either died before a year's age or were aborted. The only prognosis they could give was he might never walk, never talk, but would survive as an invalid the rest of his life. As young and naive as I was, I simply refused to believe that would be the story of Jason's life. I prayed my simple prayer again—"Lord, we need your help"—but this time I decided to believe and declare the doctor's prognosis for Jason was not going to be so.
>
> Somewhere in my little heart of hearts, I had something else rising up in me that called me to a fight. Mind you, I was not a shy person but somewhat gullible and reserved and usually believed anything anyone would tell me. But this time was different. This new confidence was not of me but a fight rising up despite my very simple faith. The feeling I had was one of defending the needs of others and not just my own child, and this point in my life was not the last time I would encounter

a challenge or believe the opposite in circumstances and sense the strength of Samson rising up in me. God intended on Jason living despite the doctors knowing nothing and us knowing nothing but us believing a great big God who loves His children and those who believe. Jason is now thirty-three years old and able to walk and talk.

At age six, Jason was enrolled in a special school for children at a time when he had only a few grunted words to express himself and mainly used simple sign language to communicate. Each year the children in the school were to have an IEP to determine their needs and their goals. He certainly had a lot of needs, but I soon found out I would need to use the "fight for their rights" approach.

I was still a very young and naive single mother. Jason's father could not handle his disabilities and so was no longer in his life. So what happened next was difficult. My son was denied speech therapy. Also, the school labeled him with behavioral issues and was ready to send him somewhere else. Even to this simple and naive mother, something just didn't make sense with this decision. It seemed as though the school was trying to get rid of Jason and me. I was shocked, surprised, and angry. I was very fortunate, however, that someone off the record pulled me aside (probably because she knew just how naive I was) and told me I had a right to appeal and where to go to get help.

At the time, I don't think the teachers knew what to do with Jason. I didn't either! He was as cute as a button but wore everyone "slap out"! He was hyperactive and could not sit still or sleep. He had a mischievous sense about him that kept everyone on constant alert, as he also did not know danger. His dry sense of humor kept us in awe and light hearted, even if for a brief moment.

I decided to appeal and went into mediation. I was led to Council for Children in Charlotte. The first step was to meet with the school's superintendent. I will never forget that day, as I had my first encounter with a giant. He used his size (I'm just 5'1") and verbal intimidation, with a tone that would normally send me running, and literally tried to back me into a corner. The Council had coached me in advance to

> hold my ground, so hold my ground I did with my knees shaking and swallowing hard in my throat a dozen times. The result was that Jason got what he deserved, which was speech therapy, and today he is able to speak and loves to talk so much that sometimes I have to turn the radio up in the car to get him to stop and just listen to the music.
>
> I can laugh now, but I sure couldn't then. This would also not be the last time I would encounter a giant. The battle for Jason's rights in education continued to be a lifelong battle, but at least I knew I had a voice to speak up and could find wisdom and council to know what direction to go in to get him help.
>
> Jason was not a simple child. Many doctors and nurses would look at me and say they didn't know what to tell me. So I just looked up where my redemption and Jason's is, and sooner or later some direction would come—not without a fight, but isn't that life? I learned that God has a redemptive purpose in everyone and opens the eyes of those who are looking.

Jason never did fit into a typical classroom, but with persistence and timing, education for children with autism came to the forefront. Jana discovered that Jason fell into a category within the autism spectrum. This helped tremendously with his education, although the school systems were still green. So Jason's education came by trial and error, but mainly by a parent's determination to stand in the gap and plow the ground where answers were not found before. Little did Jana know that in a few years, she would encounter her biggest challenge yet—and make the victory lap.

BEST RESOURCES

In an earlier chapter, the value of forgiveness and its necessity were mentioned. Romans 12:14 takes forgiveness further: "Bless those who persecute you; bless and do not curse." This verse does not mean you have to accept everything you are told and never "press back." It means you bless and pray, releasing people to God, while at the same time refusing to receive their unhealthy behavior or information as your only choice. It's not always easy, but it can be effective, as Jana and Jason's story illustrates. When you are open to new information and keep looking for the right answer, God will find a way to lead you.

Kathy, who could be constantly overwhelmed with two in a wheelchair and one with learning and focusing needs, says, "You just have to keep trusting God will lead you. Keep praying and looking for the right way to handle the situations. When you are overwhelmed and oppressed by some system, pray and wait. Keep searching. Eventually you will become better informed than most of the authorities around you because you have specialized in your child's needs."

In a networking support group, attendees can be each other's best, lion-hearted resources. When someone can't find an answer, it is strongly possibly someone else has done the homework and can help. It's amazing how specialized parents can become in networking resources that could make a quality difference in the life of children, theirs and others. Their "roar" in a group setting of like-minded others isn't heard as a loud sound but instead as solid, helpful advice.

Like them, when you become educated and experienced in helping your child with specialized needs, you too can have the roar of a passionate, persevering, hard-working parent who has uncovered some real jewels that make the difference for your family and someone else's.

ROAR TO THE HEAVENLIES

Of all the places you want your roar to be heard, the prominent one is in the heavenlies. Roar with the Word of God and the heart of God. Roar with the angels and before the hellish realm that opposes all that is good.

The best time for that kind of roar is in your prayer times. God can hear a heartbeat, even a whisper, but it's good to roar at the enemy of your soul while at the same time resting in your heavenly Father's extravagant love. Roar your declarations of God's faithfulness in the face of the evil realm as well as exclaiming God's faithfulness before the whole spiritual realm. Can you picture God's fierce angels taking a warrior's deep breath with set, determined eyes as they hear your roar, arming themselves for battle on your behalf?

Three roaring prayer parables appear in the book of Luke, chapters 11 and 18. Parables are stories that speak in comparisons and contrasts. Although each of these parables is separate, they are connected by the same theme: dispelling prayer weaknesses.

In Luke 11 is a story of a man who was traveling at night to avoid the suffocating heat. He found his way to his friend's home, where he thought he could find a respite of food and shelter. It was around midnight, and he was tired and hungry. Eastern hospitality would compel his friend to open the door and provide for the weary traveller. But instead of compassion and friendship prevailing, he was refused. Determined, the weary friend would not take no for an answer. He continued to knock and plead in a shameless pursuit of help until finally the host yielded. This story is a metaphor for perseverant prayer. It is a practical illustration of perseverant prayer being stronger than what an apathetic friend might be willing to offer.

Also in Luke 11 is the story of a strong but evil warrior who thought his victories were secure until a mightier warrior obliterated his stronghold and captured all his possessions. The evil and presumptuous warrior represents the devil. The conclusion of the story is found in verse 22. "But what if a stronger man comes along with superior weapons? Then he's beaten at his own game, the arsenal that gave him such confidence hauled off, and his precious possessions plundered" (MSG). The stronger, prevailing, victorious warrior is Jesus. Jesus Christ is the obvious Conquering Victor. By His death, burial, and resurrection, Jesus defeated the enemy and spoiled his goods, completely plundering the enemy's possessions.

As an overcomer in prayer, you are securing your victories in the heavenly realm and discovering supernatural strength from your Lord Jesus, enabling you to persevere in hard, demanding, places. You are strengthening the main frame of your identity in Christ and your dependence on His grace to enable you to do what He alone can and will empower, causing you to rise above and beyond anything you thought you could be or accomplish.

Luke 18's parable is the story of a helpless widow's faith in an impossible situation. Her faithful petitions are stronger than godlessness and injustice. The first verse is about faith that doesn't give up, ever-extending itself in prayer.

"Pray. Don't faint. Never give up." This kind of prayer, called *importunate prayer*, is the persistent, never-giving-up prayer that emerges from a mighty movement of the soul toward God.

Importunity is the ability to hold on, press on, and wait. It is restless desire with restful patience. It has a tenacious grasp and is a passion of the soul. It has a wrestling quality that does not come from physical energy. It is implanted and aroused by the Holy Spirit. Importunity is the pressing of desires with urgency and perseverance; the praying with that tenacity that doesn't give up and yet at the same time lets go.

Importunate prayer embodies shamelessness. It signifies freedom from the bashfulness that cannot ask a second time. It's a holy roar. God makes it clear in the story about the widow who never gave up that no one ever needs to be ashamed to ask or to keep on asking. The story affirms confidence in the face of intimidating people or situations that make it seem impossible to get the help needed.

STORIES OF VICTORY

Personal victory stories are powerful. As you read the story that follows, can you hear this widow roar as she presents her case? No, she's probably not rude or loud. She doesn't appear powerful in any way. She doesn't have an expert advocate at her side; nevertheless . . . Don't you just love the word *nevertheless?*

> Jesus told them a story showing that it was necessary for them to pray consistently and never quit. He said, "There was once a judge in some city who never gave God a thought and cared nothing for people. A widow in that city kept after him: "My rights are being violated. Protect me!"
>
> He never gave her the time of day. But after this went on he said to himself, "I care nothing what God thinks, even less what people think. But because this widow won't quit badgering me, I'd better do something and see that she gets justice—otherwise I'm going to end up beaten black-and-blue by her pounding."

> Then the Master said, "Do you hear what that judge, corrupt as he is, is saying? So what makes you think God won't step in and work justice for his chosen people, who continue to cry out for help? Won't he stick up for them? I assure you, he will. He will not drag his feet. But how much of that kind of persistent faith will the Son of Man find on the earth when he returns?" (Luke 18:1–8, MSG)

Keep in mind that this story, or parable, offers a contrast when it speaks of the judge. He is not like God! He is in contrast to God. God does love and care, and He doesn't fear reprisal nor does He consider your prayers badgering.

The phrase "cry out for help" in the third paragraph of the story, in the original language, means to shout for help in a tumultuous way—in other words, to roar. This woman's only weapon (tool) to fight against injustice was her roar of persistence. But you have GOD on your side, not an unjust judge! "Therefore he is able to save completely those who come to God through him, because he always lives to intercede for them" (Hebrews 7:25). Jesus lives to intercede for you. Roar!

In this parable Jesus is talking about prayerful, persistent faith in opposition. The objective for telling the story is explained in the beginning of the conversation (Luke 18:1). He wants His listeners to always pray and not give up, or as other Bible versions read, not faint. That's a more descriptive picture of the type of perseverance He's describing.

Usually one would not equate fainting with laziness. It is most common to equate fainting with being worn out from labor, stress, or weakness due to a problem. You can relate, I'm sure. It may be how you feel after your day is done. This parable shows someone who has nothing and no one to trust but her persistence and the rightness of her cause. If you are actively parenting a child with special needs, you can probably relate there as well. As an advocate for your child, the difficulties with systems or people you face aren't all brought about by injustice, but there are some that need perseverance so you can to keep on keeping on.

The parable teaches perseverance in prayer. It is not necessarily teaching continual repetition but an attitude of perseverance that keeps one in prayer. Prayers can sometimes be like kids playing ding-dong ditch, which is a game younger ones enjoy for pestering their neighbors. They run to the porch, ring the doorbell, and run. The perseverant attitude, in contrast, keeps on keeping on instead of barely hoping, praying quickly, and then running away. Waiting, when it is waiting in perseverant, trusting prayer, doesn't have to weaken your resolve. Waiting can strengthen and inspire creativity.

Widows had a prominent place in the New Testament times. In the Lord's time on earth, widows were somewhat despised and often became prey for unprincipled persons. Usually poor, they had few people, if any, to protect and deliver them. Their only hope was to come to whoever would dispense justice for intervention on their behalf. Often an object of pity, widows were mentioned in Jewish law for their helplessness. People were admonished again and again, "Do not take advantage of a widow or an orphan" (Exodus 22:22–24; Deuteronomy 10:18; 24:17). Pure religion, Jesus' disciples believed, included caring for widows in their affliction (James 1:27).

This widow was in the same town as the judge. She had been ill-treated, and she'd come to the judge for justice. Even though her cause was just, the judge paid no attention to her case. But she kept coming. Then finally, not because he cared for justice or people, but simply to get rid of the widow pestering him, he gave her what she wanted! There is power in persistence.

All that God is, the judge was not. God is exactly opposite to this judge in character and action. He is a God of compassion, comfort, and equity.

Okay, be honest here. You've probably challenged God on His definition of *quickly*. Just don't let it stop you from pressing forward. When you are tempted to give up, "Do not let your hearts be troubled and do not be afraid" (John 14:27). Truehearted souls are frequently tried by the delay of answers to prayer and are tempted to give up the praying attitude of perseverance. BE ENCOURAGED! DON'T GIVE UP! The devil hates your roar. You might want to consider the word *roar* as an acronym. ROAR: Readily Overcoming Adversarial Reasoning. Your roar alerts the angels. And God loves your roar!

The first part of Jana's story in this chapter showed her perseverance. The second part is the victory lap.

Jason, Jana, and the Powers That Be (part 2)

The new big thing was mainstreaming special needs children. The word at the time was that the school systems were going to shut all the special needs schools down and place the children in regular schools. I tried it to see if it would work, and it was a mistake. This time I was not the only parent who had a fight to defend the defenseless in them. I had a close-knit school of parents and teachers to help.

At this point I had remarried, so my husband and I and another couple decided to start an organization called PASS, which stood for Parents And Special Students. Another mother and I were on the PTA board and headed up most of the initial fight. Can you imagine two determined moms facing the school system? Not a pretty picture because we both knew who had the last say, and that was the Man upstairs. So we sent our prayers up and gathered our information and began meetings with the county superintendent. We also worked closely with ARC, the Association for Retarded Citizens.

As we stood our ground, we made the county aware of the backing we had. We had meeting after meeting with the superintendent. We listened and we spoke. We had informants give us timely information to bring to the table. It apparently became real to county officials that we were not going to stop and we had a lot of backing. The newspaper picked up the story as well. We expressed the idea of going into mediation, so they knew they had to go to their higher power, the State Superintendent.

Many times we prayed, and God provided answers, even from the school system. We learned that if you listen and keep your heart right and emotions out, you will find a way through the wilderness of the system and a structure that seemed to hold back righteousness and the needs of the people. The result was a compromise. We agreed to survey the parents, allowing them to express their concerns and questions. At the end of six months of meetings, we reached an agreement that allowed us to keep our kids in the special needs school.

Sometimes parents ask the question, "Why is this happening to me?" or "What did I do wrong to deserve this?" but don't find satisfying answers to these questions. A powerful motivating speaker, Graham Cooke, says we should not ask the why question but instead ask God, "Who do You want to be for me in this situation and what must I do?" Until we face a situation beyond ourselves, we are usually not open to the fact that not everything is about us but about who God is and how He wants to reveal Himself.

I said earlier that God has a redemptive purpose in everything, but it's up to us to find it and participate to get that redemption. Through my struggles, I am able to see not only who God is but also who He is for me in my situation and the fact that He is shows me what I need to do. He also is redeeming what was stolen from Jason's life and turning something terrible into something full of God's glory and redemption!

Now, here is the rest of Jason's God story. Later, at a ceremony at the school, the superintendent visited with Jason and me, speaking cordially to us. At the time I was carrying Jason's younger brother, Joseph, yet to be born. This man's eyes were big when he noticed, but I simply said, "Yes, I have another child coming into the system. Isn't that wonderful!"

PERSEVERING FAITH

In Luke 18, the question is asked, how much of that kind of persistent faith will the Son of Man find on the earth when He returns? An important question. It means He will be looking for those with persevering faith—still contending for the faith, still holding on and standing and believing for what is right in the midst of injustice.

Mark 11:22–24 gives a solemn charge, in spite of opposition and trials, to keep the faith—the faith of God—alive. Keep it alive in the every day activity of prayer!

God is blessing your lifestyle of trusting Him for salvation, vindication, and provision, no matter what obstacles you face. If you find yourself disappointed by personal friendships, unwilling authorities, demonic oppressions, or even ungodly injustice, your best weapon, like the widow and Jana, is to remain strong and steadfast, persevering in faith.

Love

Sometimes love roars,
    sometimes love laments,
    but love opens doors
    for God's deliverance.

Sometimes love is still,
    sometimes love is fervent,
    but love endures
    because God is omnipotent.

Love's bravery surrenders,
    esteems others higher,
    even when their needs and
    inconsiderate ways seem to try her.

Love is strong in confidence,
    and quieted in peace.
    Love knows Almighty God is Lord of all
    and gives the helpless increase.

Love's ways are caring,
    and love's manner is both forceful and tender.
    Love's reward can always be found
    in her God, who daily commends her.

PRAY

This prayer, a declaration of faith, answers Jesus' question in Luke chapter 18.

> Jesus will find faith when He comes again. No matter what I see right now, I choose to believe there will be blessed ones in abundance that hear the Word of God and keep it by remaining in faith. They will persevere to the end, trusting their God and Father. Yes, multitudes will be living in the actuated awareness of a Father-and-child relationship with God! Each believing prayer is a step nearer to the final victory. Yes, it will ripen the fruit, conquer the hindrances in the unseen world, and hasten the return of Jesus our Lord. Yes, as a child of God, I choose to give my Father time. He is long-suffering over me, and I will be long-suffering over my prayers!

All three of the parables on prayer in the book of Luke center on defeating weakness in prayer by showing where strength can be found. God is with you. Be encouraged as you persevere in a heart-surrendered communion and communication with your heavenly Father. It's time to embrace the promises of the Lord, continue in prayer, and fight the good fight of faith with a holy roar ascending into heaven's realm.

REFLECT

1. In what have you persevered in prayer and seen God intervene in the outcome?

2. What prayer of faith is in your mind right now, not yet formulated into a roar?

10

Stalwart Seeds Grow Anywhere: Is It Spring Yet?

From disappointment, condemnation, and dissatisfaction to gratefulness, praise, and contentment

FOCUSED, HARD-WORKING PARENTS find themselves researching, researching, and researching again for the answers they need. They do whatever it takes so that their child's life can be like a healthy, growing garden. They long for an abundant harvest for the ones they love. They'll do just about anything to optimize their child's garden potential. The *settling* stage is long, and without much warning it can spiral back to feelings of earlier stages of *surviving* and *searching*.

When the research of the *settling* stage continuously causes hard-working parents to compare their child to a myriad of others with the same diagnosis or similar need, it can cause their hope for that garden to shrivel. The home front weather changes from warm, sunshiny days sprinkled with soft rain to an impending, severe cold front. The atmospheric pressure drops, and the wind gets stronger as the cold front reaches into their soul, drastically lowering the emotional temperature. The extreme cold of an icy winter looms ahead—again. How are the healthy seeds ever going to flourish?

SEEDS OF DISCONTENTMENT

The urge to continually compare your child's progress to the progress of others can crowd the good soil you've planted with seeds of discontent. Constant comparisons can become a formidable enemy to your contentment. Many parents lose all of the ground they fought to clear. The truth is that what's gone is the past. What remains might seem like nothing more than tiny seeds, but they are the kernels to start planting again.

Focusing on even the smallest evidence of something good, not on what was lost, is transformational. Unsure? Of course, so was God's mighty warrior Gideon until God changed his mind, altering his experience.

Read the story of Marvie and her daughter, and see what happened as she compared her situation to a neighbor's, allowing seeds of discontentment to grow.

Marvie's Tears

> Marvie has a four-year-old daughter, Alicia, with severe mental and physical weaknesses. She thrashes from side to side when she's attempting to communicate. During those times, only her mom or dad have any idea what she needs or wants. Marvie and her husband can read some of their daughter's grunts and signs, but most of the time, they too are just perplexed.
>
> In the beginning, tears flowed down their cheeks as they watched Alicia's attempts and obvious frustration at the task at hand. After all, their neighbor down the street was a parent of a child with a similar diagnosis, and compared to the neighbors' progress, Marvie felt like she and her husband lagged a distance behind. Exhaustion and fear began to hold hands, dragging Alicia's parents into a spiraling depression that culminated in a fatalistic resignation.
>
> Sitting in the chair, alone in the living room, Marvie would stare into nothingness, and then with her whole body heaving, she would have spurts of what she referred to as convulse crying. Speaking to herself, she would attempt to transition into a calmer response with a

> stern reprimand, "What do you think you're doing, Marvie? Stop crying. What good is it going to do? Just stop it." She saw no value in her tears and doubted she would ever taste contentment again.

Marvie's case is extreme, but it does point out that comparison and the resulting self-condemnation can be dangerous. But the tears themselves are not the problem. When tears come, and they will, it's good to remember that all tears aren't bad. They can have a very positive, watering effect in your family's life. When tears come, please know that you aren't necessarily losing your grip.

When a grapevine is pruned, the sap that seeps from its cuts can look like the vine is crying. A friend, Cindy Steinbeck, author of *The Vine Speaks*, shared with me her observation about pruning. The sap is the energy, the life of the vine flowing from the wound made by pruning sheers. The woundedness speaks loudly, but so does the energy flowing from the vine. Christ's life works in us and through us, even when we don't have energy to continue on. His life is alive in us. Ephesians 3:20–21 says, "Now to him who is able to do immeasurably more than all we ask or imagine, according to his power that is at work within us, to him be glory in the church and in Christ Jesus throughout all generations, forever and ever! Amen."

TEARS COMMUNICATE

It's natural to cry. It's healthy to cry now and again. It's common to have a few hours or days moving forward in a state of peaceful contentment and then kaboom, crash, down you go, exasperated by the realities that bring havoc, heartache, pain, thrashing behavior, and panic-stricken need. It's wearing, to be sure! Once again, your inner being screams, "I'm not cut out for this! This isn't fair!" Once again, tears fill your eyes.

Most people feel better after crying. It's therapeutic. If you search the Web for the word *tears,* you will find some interesting statistics. People generally feel calmer, more relaxed after crying. Tears can be healing and restorative. Often tears are a way to grieve and let go, move on in the process, and change perspective. After crying, it's common to feel like wanting to lie down and rest.

The need is real. When was the last time you had a good cry? How did it make you feel?

It's good to know that tears don't have to dissolve contentment but instead aid it. Another word for *contentment* is *sufficiency*. During life-threatening trials or deep disappointments, it is possible to experience a growing sufficiency for handling crises. Apostle Paul wrote, "I know what it is to be in need, and I know what it is to have plenty. I have learned the secret of being content in any and every situation, whether well fed or hungry, whether living in plenty or in want" (Philippians 4:12). It's true that he wasn't a parent; but his needs were life threatening, and his discoveries are valid for anyone.

Tears are God's resource to humans for emotional release and prayerful statement. Psalm 126:5 comforts us with these words: "Those who sow with tears will reap with songs of joy." Tears communicate. They can be signals not only to you but to the ones present during your tearful times.

Most importantly, God sees your tears and considers your situation. Jesus tearfully prayed, expressing His longing for God's family to love one another deeply and make the kind of choices that would bring life, beauty, and blessing. Hebrews 5:7 gives a peek into Jesus' prayer life: "During the days of Jesus' life on earth, he offered up prayers and petitions with fervent cries and tears to the one who could save him from death, and he was heard because of his reverent submission."

Jesus fervently cried in deep concern for those He came to save, deliver, heal, and bring back into a healthy, loving relationship with God the Father in heaven. The shortest verse in the Bible (John 11:35) states, "Jesus wept," and says no more. He cried and He was heard. You cry and you are heard.

Apostle Paul describes his life serving God as one of great suffering, and often tears flowed with deep, heartfelt love for the people. Acts 20:19 records these words: "I served the Lord with great humility and with tears and in the midst of severe testing." King David, in Psalm 56:8, cries out to God, "Record my misery; list my tears on your scroll—are they not in your record?"

Therapist Michelle Phillips emphasizes the heartfelt love in these verses. "The tears from Jesus and Paul reference their tears of sorrow for others. Parents sometimes cry out of love for their child when they see the child's suffering. Other times they cry for themselves, their own lost dreams, the burden of care, or the variety of deep emotional responses. God heals in both cases."

Tears make a difference. Your tears are recorded in heaven. Don't let them simply water the unwanted seeds of discontentment. Give them to your Father in heaven. He will use them for good.

THE DANGER OF UNCHECKED COMPARISON

Therapist Michelle Phillips notes that in the Bible are many psalms David wrote that use comparisons. "David (a man after God's own heart) had a problem with comparison. Many of the psalms start with 'Why, God?' but end with praise as David's perspective changes. Isn't that the secret to contentment, to move away from 'It's useless to serve God' to 'I have a commission from on high'? and 'With every breath He gives, I will serve the Lord'? I've learned that everything God gave me, my strengths and weaknesses, are given to complete my unique calling."

Malachi 3:14–15 records the prophet Malachi's response to what people were saying that displeased God, their comparisons sowing seeds of discontentment. "You have said, 'It is futile to serve God. What do we gain by carrying out his requirements and going about like mourners before the LORD Almighty? But now we call the arrogant blessed. Certainly evildoers prosper, and even when they put God to the test, they get away with it.'"

The people of Malachi's time were comparing their lives with those around them. Their attitude was based on these comparisons and what they perceived instead of what God revealed. Their comparisons led them to the wrong conclusions. God sees. God hears. God cares.

It happens. From time to time, you compare your parenting to the rest of your friends. You feel like you trudge it out day by day for someone who may have little or no comprehension of your sacrifice. All parents are unappreciated to some extent, but parents of children with special needs feel the anonymity more acutely. Ignored. Not appreciated. No one has a clue. So much is done behind the scenes. Is it worth it? How much is enough? Will it ever end? Can a person truly find contentment spending hour upon hour doing multitudes of unending, detailed, monotonous tasks?

Your situation just doesn't seem fair. Life *does* have many inequities and enigmas. The question is, what to do about it? Does this nagging awareness become an enemy of the badge of honor that only you and your heavenly Father know about? Probably, but you can overcome this perspective (Romans 8:18; 2 Corinthians 4:17; 10:12).

Melanie described how she went from extreme challenge to a rewarding honor.

> Mostly for me it was others that seemed to compare my parenting against their own parenting of typical children. And my parenting always came up short when using my children's behaviors as the measuring stick. But every once in awhile, I would wonder about how my own inadequacies contributed to the lack of development that I could easily discern in my children, especially their spiritual development.
>
> My girlfriend shared with me about praying with her sons about their academic options. Her description of their earnestness was something I wanted to rejoice with her in, but instead I found myself comparing my daughter's bitterness against God for not healing her. And I compared my son's desperate need for acceptance by his peers that trumped his spiritual hunger in a way that my input could not compete.
>
> My girlfriend's story brought me pain that threatened to bury me in shame. The comparison not only devalued my own efforts, but also trivialized my children's own progression of faith. Eventually I came to an important realization. Although their development looked very different, their faith journey was equally as poignant.
>
> The fruit of pondering is the revelation of the nature of the root. When you can recognize the spiral of demoralization and shame, it's time to do some thought weeding to remove the comparison and rejoice over your own little mini victories. After all, Scripture teaches that although it was Paul that planted and Apollos that watered, it was God who gave the increase.

Comparisons can be a tremendous challenge to overcome. Consider these lines of a Christian song that encourages those who can't figure out what's going on: "When you can't trace His hand, trust His heart." Yes, you pray for a miracle and God's best. At the same time, it's imperative to learn how to find contentment without comparison as you continue to love and serve your child. Yes, it is worthwhile. Yes, it is rewarding.

Therapist Michelle Phillips gives a word of advice and a story.

> One way to avoid unchecked comparisons is to watch associations. Choose friends wisely. I know stories of people who God has used amazingly. One: Matthew was born with cerebral palsy and intellectual disabilities. His parents (pastors) were encouraged to place him in an institution. Instead they kept him as part of their family and part of the church family. In the early years, many prayed for his healing.
>
> Matthew had a special talent. He could remember people's names and the date he met them. He would stop people and ask, "Who's number one?" and not let them go until they said, "Jesus is number one." And, at times, he would remind people to pray. He often told people, "Pray for Bob and Michelle."
>
> When he passed as the result of a seizure in his 20s, the church was filled to overflowing with people who had known him over the years. Truly, I think he touched more people significantly in his life than I could hope to touch.

In the story in the book of Malachi, the people were comparing themselves with those they felt weren't serving God, jealous of what was happening in their lives. Their hard feelings grew into discontented complaining. Their comparisons drew the conclusion that the undeserving were enjoying life's pleasures more than they were. Their discord, anger, and resentment were displeasing to God.

Apostle Paul in Galatians 5:25–26 warns against comparisons, saying, "Since we live by the Spirit, let us keep in step with the Spirit. Let us not become conceited, provoking and envying each other."

To this thought therapist Michelle Phillips adds, "God doesn't look at the magnitude of our accomplishments in the way the world does, in the way we do sometimes. He looks at our faithfulness to the task He has given us."

As the value of your eternal "hidden badge of honor" increases, the need to look for honors and popularity from your peers will decrease, causing your sense of contentment to grow. What a relief!

Contentment is rooted in the soil of grace. Grace is God's unmerited favor, a gift of His Spirit you can't earn or learn. It's His empowering presence, enabling you to become a man or woman of an excellent spirit. By His grace, His empowering presence, you are enabled to be what He has called you to be. It's favor you haven't earned, and it's ability beyond your own. It enables a reliance on the Unseen Himself.

Life *isn't* fair. Contentment is. It's the opposite of comparison.

DETERMINATION OF VALUE

How do you determine value? Society says that a person is valuable *if*, with a long list of accomplishments after the *if*. The temptation to see your child with developmental needs as severely lacking and displeasing is natural. Do these comparisons open the door for you to think, "What good is it to serve God *if* this is all I get in return?"

You're still not going to always say just the right thing from the perfect motivation. Remember, God forgives your worst grumbling, even when your tongue lashes out at Him. Just ask.

You are extremely valuable. He loves you with an everlasting love. You may be disappointed or sad, but avoid allowing yourself and your perspective on your child to be wounded permanently by comparisons. Grace will enable you to see what God sees and value what He values. Your growing peace and contentment, as a result, will astound your friends as you serve and love, no matter how many needs your child has in comparison to other families. Most importantly, heaven rejoices in your choice.

When comparisons determine that others seem to have it so much better, Kerry says she takes a big breath and searches for another thought—a healthier one. "I cry out to God. I say, 'Help, Holy Spirit. I choose Your viewpoint. Help me plant the quality choice to bypass these unhealthy soul reactions.' It's unexplainable how He makes the difference. In faith, by prayer and thanksgiving, I am learning to trust the living waters of the Holy Spirit to help me and lead me into the 'peace that passes understanding' (Philippians 4:7) and the 'godliness with contentment' that brings great gain (1 Timothy 6:6)."

ATTITUDE OF GRATITUDE

"Really? I thought I was done with this! Here I go again," Gary said with a sigh. "If you are at all like me, when you are overwhelmed, you might blurt out rash, negative statements. You mean what you say, at least for that moment. Later, you come to the conclusion that rash negativity has not only no benefit but steals from you more than you are willing to do without."

Chuck and Melanie, parents of two children with special needs, share their external and internal attitude adjustments.

> Chuck:
> As Dad, I can think of multiple times I've blown it with the children. For example, on those occasions when our son would speak disrespectfully to my wife, it incensed me. My wife and I agreed in advance how to calmly handle conflict situations like this, yet I still managed to come in like a cawing, swooping eagle, creating ineffective resolution and devastating defeat, having blown it yet again. In reflecting on how I handled the situations in the aftermath, I had to own how and where I crossed the line. I can't think of a case where I didn't go back to eat crow afterward to my children, explaining that Daddy blew it. I have made "Will you please forgive me?" a redemptive part of my parenting, not just saying the simpler phrase, "I'm sorry." The result is that I have been able to make peace with myself, even in the midst of my perceived failures.

Melanie:

I have learned the extreme value of disciplining my mouth. I believe our words send angels on assignment. Our words can affect the quality of life or bring a death sentence, invading the potential for the family's well-being. Our words align heaven with earth. I covenanted long ago to use my words oh so carefully while bringing correction in the midst of overwhelm. My temperament is a controlled one, and I struggle more with leading with my mind devoid of heart than I do with blowing it with my emotions and mouth.

Do you recall the children's poem that chanted, "Mary, Mary quite contrary, how does your garden grow?" In the poem Mary's garden grew "silver bells, cockleshells, and pretty maids all in a row." Reality says, "I don't think so!" The true answer to the question of what grows in Mary's garden would be more like, "Barely anything at all." Contrary attitudes grow only conflict and incompatible responses (Galatians 5:17).

Each of the stories in this chapter reveals that planting seeds of discontentment with yourself or others doesn't produce anything good and neutralizes your God-given ability to excel. A stalwart seed is a seed that finds its nourishment from heavenly resources and therefore can grow a strong healthy crop of gratitude nurturing contentment.

Contentment is not just an illusive butterfly. It is attainable. You have chosen to embrace the identity transitions, tears and all. You know that the deeper experience of God's grace is an ongoing journey. The significance of that journey is emerging. It's becoming more rewarding, truly worthwhile, even when you have setbacks, make comparisons, and grumble. Even if you don't feel it now, you can anticipate the positive, that one day you will find yourself referring to parenting as a privilege, one backed by an attitude of gratitude. With a little inward grin and a grateful heart, you'll recognize new growth breaking through the soil. When it happens, it is perception altering, transforming. Your awakened heart will find gratefulness hidden in the crevices of every day life.

The book *One Thousand Gifts* by Ann Voskamp is a dare to live fully, right where you are. It gives insights in how to open the door into the miracle of holy joy through finding gratitude in neutral, everyday, and natural places. When you embrace it, your sense of the value of life will broaden as you dip into the wealth a grateful attitude offers. Each attitude of gratitude, each grateful inspired grin, plants seeds—strong, incorruptible, prize-winning seeds in your soul's garden.

You and your child are valuable children in the family of God with an eternal divine purpose and destiny. You as the parent are growing in a dynamic transformation process. That old saying, bloom where you are planted, is showing you your own personal garden spot. Of course, every garden has weeds, days of draught, and sometimes overwatering. An experienced gardener who tenderly watches over the plants makes all the difference in the health and beauty of the garden life. Trust Him.

James 5:7 says, "Be patient, then, brothers and sisters, until the Lord's coming. See how the farmer waits for the land to yield its valuable crop, patiently waiting for the autumn and spring rains." John 15:1 says, "I am the true vine and my Father is the gardener."

In 2 Timothy 2, Paul encourages Timothy to face his battles by using several metaphors Timothy would understand. Paul talks about being a good soldier and a great athlete and then tells Timothy to start thinking like a farmer. Timothy knows farming is strenuous work. Paul then gives him a promise for the end of the day in verse 6: "The hardworking farmer should be the first to receive a share of the crops."

There's a reward coming. If you have done any farming yourself, you know it can be a thankless job for many months until those first sprouts begin to peek above the ground. Okay, you may plow a crooked row now and then in your attitude, but your goal is to keep on keeping on doing what you know to do in the best you know how to do it. This Scripture is God's personal promise to Timothy that as he puts his hand to the plow and works hard, a reward will be coming. That promise is His special promise to you too.

God's grace and forgiveness in Christ has room for negative attitudes and words when you're in emotional pain or confusion. God reads the heart beyond the words. He understands your desperate pleas for answers. Remember, He is not sitting in heaven holding a judgmental bat, just ready to swing at you if you say or do something displeasing to Him. At the same time, He knows the personal benefits available when you come into agreement with His words, His ways, and the value of His sacrifice. Jesus is the example. Think about what He sacrificed to draw you into God's close-knit family.

Make no mistake about it—your parenting is an act of serving, honoring, and loving God! God values what you do and records the sacrifices, suffering, and hard work. You are a sweet smelling fragrance, a bright light of His glory, and an obvious example of His goodness as you daily serve Him by loving your child, planting those life-giving, stalwart seeds of serving in faith, hope, and love.

Your rewards are forthcoming and everlasting. Colossians 3:24 reminds you, saying, "Since you know that you will receive an inheritance from the Lord as a reward. It is the Lord Christ you are serving." Matthew 6:4b says, "Then your Father, who sees what is done in secret, will reward you." (Matthew 6:4; 6:18.)

REVEALED SECRET

Humankind was created to live in an eternal, incredibly beautiful garden the Bible names the Garden of Eden. No wonder nature and its extravagant beauty ministers to our soul. We were originally formed to live out our days in the exquisite fragrance and lavish colors of a magnificent garden.

The fact that life is eternal brings a huge paradigm shift in assigning value to daily tasks. What is insignificant or even worse, pitied by some is honored and prized by your heavenly Father, His Son Jesus, and your comforting guide, the Holy Spirit. Your acts of love done in secret are precious to God and others with a heart of understanding.

His empowering presence is what makes the difference. That's grace. The disappointments are real, and yet they don't disfigure deeply rooted contentment. Connie's story points to the revealed secret.

The Garden

> Connie's family decided to plant a garden with radishes, carrots, corn, lettuce, tomatoes, and spinach. Her son, Walter, was so excited as he dug each tiny hole with his little hands, just the right size for the seed. Every day for a week he begged his mom to go out and see if anything was growing. Of course, all the growth was still underground.
>
> One day little Walter snuck out past the gate into the garden. He could see the little green tops of the carrots and radishes at last poking through the soil. Carefully he tiptoed between the rows, looking over his shoulder every few minutes. He pulled up a radish green top to peek at its progress. Nope, nothing but a scrawny little red thing that certainly didn't look like a radish. He then pulled up the green top of a carrot, and its root looked more like a scrawny orange string. Nothing anyone could eat.
>
> Now what? They needed more time in the soil. So Walter buried them once again, thinking they could finish growing until one day he would eat big, fat, yummy veggies.
>
> It didn't happen. His impatient pulling up of those two tender vegetables-to-be stopped their growth. Impatient Walter had a few less radishes and carrots to enjoy.

It's definitely a temptation to wonder about the seed. How long is it going to take to show fruit? But count on it. Something healthy is growing beneath the surface. You are being transformed. Are you convinced yet? Given time, little sprouts begin to appear. Internal stability, calming the soul in peaceful contentment, is ripening even when nothing on the outside can be seen. You will get to taste its bounty. Keep planting your healthy seeds, and give God's peace and multiplied grace time to grow. Stalwart seeds can grow, producing a delicious, nourishing crop anywhere.

The Stalwart Seed

Will you look at that!
Unbelievable!
How could that flower grow
In such a tiny crack?
Why, there isn't even any room
And yet, just look at it bloom.

I bet you nothing could impede
That stalwart little seed.
I guess it found a small shaft of light
And pushed its way.
What a sight!

HOW TO GROW CONTENTMENT

God's desire to give you significant measures of His personal peace is beyond your imagination. Again, it is a gift, but it also grows with practice. Philippians 4:7 says, "And the peace of God, which transcends all understanding, will guard your hearts and your minds in Christ Jesus." Philippians 4:9 says, "Whatever you have learned or received or heard from me, or seen in me—put it into practice. And the God of peace will be with you."

Hothouse in Spring

The most meaningful springtime you will ever know
is the one that blooms in the hothouse surrounded by snow.
Its yield knows not the exterior's cold lament
but instead profusely thrives with a sweet-smelling scent.
(Jesus was and is the earthly precedent.)

The measure of its beauty shall never wither or fade.
It remains safe from the temperature's every whim and cannonade.
The hothouse stands, as someone once coined the phrase,
"in the dead of winter" as a serenade.

And yet within the length of these cold, harsh days
You can see plants and flowers on display.
Yes, it's a fair and wonderful thing
This hothouse filled with spring.

Kerry was sure there just had to be a way to grow contentment in the midst of her parenting challenges. In her research, she discovered peace was contentment's faithful sidekick and friend. It seemed logical they would grow together. As a matter of fact, she referred to contentment and peace as jolly good friends.

She went searching for their sage advice. She read books and poetry. She spent time with calming landscape paintings and considerable time reading the Scriptures about peace and contentment. One day as she jotted down her meditations, an imbedded "aha" emerged to quiet her angst and soothe her longings. She wrote:

Peace is learned.
But isn't peace a gift from God?
Yes.
How are both true?
Learned, not earned.
Peace is an occupation of the soul and spirit,
A weapon that can be depended on.
Its battle scars are seen below the surface.
Peace is both a gift and process.
It is nourished during relationship with God in sweet fellowship.
What is fellowship?
Fellowship is fellow heirs, fellow citizens,
and fellow friends responding to the God of creation.
Peace is born of understanding
    fathered by patience;
    mothered by hope;
    nurtured in faith;
    and trained in wisdom.
Contentment and peace are best friends.
Their overshadowing perspective of the eternal spirit builds a haven of rest.
Ahhhh, that's peace God's way.
That's heavenly contentment on earth as it is in heaven.

Serving may not feel like a glorious life, especially during those monotonous, repetitive times. But to your heavenly Father, it reveals His love to humankind. It's in the DNA code of your spirit, brilliant and eternally rewarding.

Servanthood

Servanthood in Christ is a dignity and a delight.
It is the torch He carries, the cloud by day, the fire by night.
While many in this day are saying that it's none of their affair,
our Lord Jesus desires that we reach out and show we care.

Don't inherit the winds of judgmental or apathetic attitudes,
blowing dust in the face of need,
but instead let the mighty rushing wind of God's compassion
be your motivating force and creed.
Parenting from a servant's heart
has less to say than it does to impart.

In heaven's hall of fame is carved each servant's name.
Is it the price of entrance?
No, only a kind recognition of significance.
Jesus said, "What you have done unto the least of these,
you've done unto Me."

As you serve and love and care for your child,
your Lord takes it quite personally.
God's not as interested in what shows
as He is in what goes on when no one else knows.

Serving hearts have eyes to see and ears to hear
what the Spirit of Christ desires and holds dear.
So let our Lord Jesus' humble and loving ways
captivate your heart and delight your days.

PRAY

Father God, help me have a healthier mind as I process life's many extreme challenges that tempt me toward disfiguring attitudes that lead to grumbling, jealousy of others, bitterness, weakness, disappointment, and the upheaval of emotional volcanoes. I believe the blood of Jesus cleanses me of the negative effects of my responses as I ask Him, and I am thankful for forgiveness and cleansing once again. I choose to follow the leading of the Holy Spirit, Lord, and trust His empowering to make my life fruit bearing.

What a thought, Lord. I look forward to feeling fruitful about my life and myself. I look forward to growing in Your personal equipping measure of glory. What a gift. You are beautifying my garden. Help me to value what I do with Your perspective and find contentment watering my own. I claim the words of Psalm 19:14, "May these words of my mouth and this meditation of my heart be pleasing in your sight, Lord, my Rock and my Redeemer."

REFLECT

1. What stalwart seeds of faith, hope, or love are you planning to plant today?

2. What small delights have superseded the rough edges of a stressful time?

3. What joys have surprised you recently?

11

Laughter of Grace: What Just Happened?

From exasperation, depletion, and raw raging reactions to grace enabled, healthy emotions with the occasional added ingredient of humor

Some languages don't have separate words to express the difference between *happiness* and *joy*. When people talk about happiness, they often refer to outward pleasing circumstances. Joy, instead, is reserved for a settled, peaceful, trusting, emotional stability that serves as a foundation to happiness.

Depending on the Bible version you read, the two words can be used interchangeably. Joy is the presence and power of God living in you and expressing His strength and pleasure through your emotions. It's a divine impartation. Joy is stronger and deeper than happiness that comes as a result of something good that happened. Joy doesn't always feel like fun or laughter, yet it can readily be expressed in laughter.

Grace is God's empowering enablement. It takes you beyond your own abilities. It enables the activation of God-given joy. Living from the reservoir of God's grace makes it possible to find yourself humming a light-hearted, internal melody or breaking out in bursts of laughter right smack dab in the middle of dilemma, distress, or disillusionment.

He who laughs often lasts and lasts. It is rumored that Red Buttons, an 80-year-old comedian at the time, said his longevity was due to humor and health foods. "Eighty is not old," he told people. "Old is when your doctor no longer X-rays you; he just holds you up to the light. That's old. Old is when you order a two-minute egg and they ask you to pay in advance. Learning to laugh at yourself develops patience and a great tolerance for frustration and zaps you with a jolly good time."

A merry heart, laughter, and joy all dispense a large dose of medicinal aid to a weary soul. Oh, what a delight when laughter is spontaneous, lifting your whole being into cheerful delight!

Jesus asked His followers to "be of good cheer." Faith and good humor are powerful healing friends. Your faith has been building steadily, but have you discovered the healing power of a good belly laugh yet? If not, your time is coming. It's your turn.

FIND THE BALANCE

Jan blew it. She saw her boss working diligently week after week in emotional and physical caretaking. One day she bought him a Christian joke book, wrote a little friendly note inside, and mailed it off to him, thinking she had done a kind thing.

"I'm sure you could use a laugh and some pleasurable moments in all your hard work," was all she wrote.

The phone rang a few days later. Her leader was very upset. "With everything else I have to deal with, you dare to write me a note saying I don't know how to have a good time and don't know how to laugh!"

Shock. "Oh, my goodness, I am so sorry. I only meant to give you a gift to honor your hard work. I wasn't accusing you, only attempting to lighten your day."

Silence. "Okay, just remember my perspective when I read these words. I will choose to believe you, but next time watch out how you say it. Thank you for the thought."

Sometimes a situation is so intense that even the best intentions to lighten it are missed. Proverbs 27:14 says, "If anyone loudly blesses their neighbor early in the morning, it will be taken as a curse." Of course morning is not the only time someone's good intentions are misunderstood. It can happen at any time of the day, the week, or the season, especially so when you are under intense stress.

Proverbs 15 gives an intriguing description of a merry heart as hopeful, definitely positive, and inviting. "A happy heart makes the face cheerful, but heartache crushes the spirit. The discerning heart seeks knowledge, but the mouth of a fool feeds on folly. All the days of the oppressed are wretched, but the cheerful heart has a continual feast" (verses 13–15). Can you imagine the tasty delicacies available to those with a cheerful heart? In contrast, 1 Peter 4:7 records the value of being sober and alert for the purpose of prayer.

Be sober and alert. Have a merry heart. How can both alert sobriety and cheerfulness live in the same heart at the same time?

CHOOSE JOY

There is unity in what may seem to be opposites. Admittedly, soberness and alertness seem to come more naturally in difficult or confusing times than a jovial, cheery heart. So sometimes it takes a deliberate choice to act on positive thoughts and divine truths that engender lighthearted merriment before one can engage in cheerfulness.

Cheerfulness in the Lord isn't a blind, flighty foolishness. Sober thinking isn't necessarily somber, melancholy, or dull but clear headed, temperate, and restrained in its considerations. Someone with a merry, cheerful heart isn't an oblivious person in denial but instead can be someone with a positive, lively hope that has been activated by faith in God's perspectives regarding life. Both merry and somber are valuable attributes to take with you on your journey. When you experience them working together, it's usually a surprise, one that reveals a strong sense of completeness, balance, and full centeredness.

Good humor is infectious, and a good-humored person changes the atmosphere of a room. You probably have experienced a time when the sound of thunderous laughter or even snickering was far more contagious than a cough or sneeze. When laughter is shared, people feel closer to each other. There is an increased feeling of happiness that opens the door to a form of intimacy. Laughter connects you to others.

There are physical reasons everyone should pursue a merry heart. Laughter triggers healthy physical changes in the body. Humor and laughter make you more alert, strengthen your immune system, boost your energy, diminish pain, and help lessen the damaging effects of stress. A good laugh can relax the whole body, and most people enjoy the fact it burns calories. It releases endorphins, the body's natural feel-good chemical, and promotes an overall sense of well-being.

Doctors have observed that laughing is good exercise for the lungs, heart, diaphragm, and stomach, helping circulation by clearing toxins from the respiratory system. It protects the heart by improving the function of the blood vessels and increasing blood flow. It is your body's natural antidote for stress, pain, and conflict. Some say nothing works faster or more dependably to bring your mind and body back into a healthy balance than a good laugh.

No wonder God's Word has volumes to say about joy, a merry heart, and laughter. Nehemiah 8:10 declares, "The joy of the LORD is your strength."

Beth was impressed by the wisdom of an older mom's counsel. First she explained how the joy of the Lord could be Beth's personal strength. Then the woman added, "And your joy is to be your child's strength." That insight opened the door to a new perspective for Beth. Her child's stubborn refusals and unwillingness to comply with the needed training was draining. It made her feel rejected by those she was serving and loved dearly. The thought that her children could benefit from her personal joy or laughter wasn't completely foreign, but she hadn't thought of her joy as something that would give them strength.

She began to wonder, *Is joy a choice? Is laughter or a merry heart a choice?* She had always believed they must come spontaneously, but she began to rethink that premise. She was already a follower of Jesus. She believed the Holy Spirit gave her inner resources beyond the natural she could strive to produce. But it began to dawn on her that this inner provision of the Holy Spirit, a merry heart, could possibly be a reservoir of joy.

She had a new resolve to draw her joy and even a good belly laugh from Him instead of expecting her children to be her source for joy. At least on occasion, she would choose to let a merry heart and laughter "bubble up" from within. After she began to practice this focus, she found a surprising measure of relief from her raw or raging reactions. Her emotional life became less frantic and upset.

It may sound like an odd exercise, but she actually set aside practice times for joy, a merry heart, and laughter. When it seemed almost impossible to tap into the hopeful, cheerful, inner realm of God's personal presence, she would get out a good clean joke book or put on one of her favorite DVDs to make her at least smile or maybe even laugh out loud. This act primed her pump until she could focus on something pleasant and holistically helpful for the task at hand.

Over time, she discovered that the joy of the Lord not only changed her on the inside but also began to make a difference in how her child responded to her instructions. Through her exercise, she was learning how to draw from the deep provisions available in the saving graces of her Lord. Jesus was more than her God who had washed away her sin and cleansed her of all unrighteousness. He was her personal Lord and God, and His goodness was her greatest source for joy. This verse testified to her experience.

Isaiah 12:3, "With joy you will draw water from the wells of salvation."

"Laughing and playing with Joey caused double takes as people passed by us," Susan shared. "At first I wondered why. What was the oddity that caused them to look again or stare, watching my son and me laughing together? We were having a good time. It all seemed normal to me.

"Then I realized what it was. We were laughing, and the onlookers thought there couldn't be any happiness when a child had special needs like my son did. They were surprised. Our joy just didn't fit their idea of 'normal.' When I came to that realization, it caused an inner grin. My son and I had a secret together: life can be a beautiful, happy time when you see each other through God's eyes, His heart, and the joy of knowing His plan."

Proverbs 14:30 says, "A heart at peace gives life to the body." Susan had discovered the truth of this proverb, and those who saw her joy wanted to understand it.

June's experience was more like an inner calm that softened the wrinkles on her face. She said finding a place of peace, let alone joy, was difficult for a long while. She had a constant, inward, sick feeling. Her energy zapped, she felt continually less than—not equal to the task—and her face mirrored it. It was an act of trust when she decided, "I am going to quote until I believe Proverbs 14:30 and other words on peace and joy from the Bible." What she chose to do wasn't just positive thinking. It was more. It was positive believing that she had invited the Holy Spirit into her heart and therefore His presence could be, would be more. It would be life to her body.

Yes, it took time, but June says the wait was worth it in the end. Her intentional merry heart began to have a physical effect on her whole being. She was restored to her real self she thought was hiding in there somewhere. She was the June she used to be. But there was an even bigger surprise. She was a better June, as only God Himself could inspire and renew. Psalm 146:5 (NLT) was her testimony: "But joyful are those who have the God of Israel as their helper, whose hope is in the LORD their God."

Pat experienced the icing on the cake of joy, a fresh measure of happiness. It emerged from the help she was receiving from caring friends and was strengthened by the hope she was nurturing. And no one could deny the difference. Her face told the truth. She began to have a radiant look that brought joy to everyone's heart.

Pat's change started before a circumstance turned around for the better, even before she had a large dose of time to just get used to the new challenge. It was in the midst of difficulties and during the health issues that she began to notice the difference. Her friends had been asking about the changes they could see, but she couldn't tell any difference at first. The change in her was small but incremental, until she started noticing a restored vibrancy. God was working His work of renewing the inward person in her (Proverbs 15:30; 16:24; 2 Corinthians 4:16). The words of Solomon in Proverbs 16:20 (AMP) became her reality: ""He who deals wisely and heeds [God's] word and counsel shall find good, and whoever leans on, trusts in, and is confident in the Lord—happy, blessed, and fortunate is he."

PRACTICE SOME LAUGHTER

Life without times of happiness, joy, and robust laughter can be a long, laborious mass of exertion, as you well know. Of course there are appropriate times for sober, serious considerations, but joy can be the undercurrent. Today, while you are reading, consider stepping into a "merry heart break," at least for a few minutes. Like taking a walk out of a busy kitchen or a home restoration project, your break can become a mental stroll into a beautiful garden with bright flowers and a sweet scent in the air.

It's time for newness of life to spring forth. Think on these things, says the Bible. "Finally, brothers and sisters, whatever is true, whatever is noble, whatever is right, whatever is pure, whatever is lovely, whatever is admirable—if anything is excellent or praiseworthy—think about such things" (Philippians 4:8). Read Janet's discovery that laughter could break through a spell of misery.

Laughter Broke the Spell

Janet took the kids on a long car trip to see the relatives. Coming home, she encountered construction seemingly everywhere on the freeways. Detour signs again and again caused her to change lanes and confused her travel directions. The next thing she knew, she was lost. Out came the old map Mama had given her for the trip. It was before cell phones and GPSs could give directions.

The kids were pinching and picking at each other, complaining and whining in the back seat. They had been in the car for eight hours, and young ADHD was kicking the seat. Teener was yelling at ADHD, "Cut it out!" Little one was crying in the car seat again when she heard Janet lament with a deep sigh at being lost again. It was car chaos.

The scene kept getting worse until driver mom pulled over in sheer exasperation. It was late, dark, and she was lost, trying desperately to read the map and look for the local signs to see where to go. Teener and mom driver were huddled together around the flashlight, hunting for anything familiar on the map, when ADHD unbuckled, reached across the seat, and grabbed the map. A large chunk ripped out of the middle into ADHD's hands.

Everyone just stared for a moment. The map was now useless with a large hole right where driver mom and teener had been searching.

> But it wasn't hardly a second until the whole situation seemed hysterically funny to everyone but little one in the car seat. The laughter burst open. Driver mom and the older two laughed so hard tears rolled down their faces. Little one sat quietly, trying to figure out what just happened as all of the anger, frustration, fear, and emotional upheaval that could be imagined to fill a setting like this one dissipated. The car was calmer now. Even ADHD was just wiggling instead of slamming into the seat. Little one was sniffling softly.
>
> "Okay kids, what shall we do?" driver mom asked. Little one, still a bit tearful whispered, "I want to go home NOW." Teener and ADHD suggested, "Let's just find a hotel."
>
> Driver mom started the car again and headed for the nearest side street to find the much-needed resting place. As they pulled up to the first motel, little one started to cry again, saying, "No, Mom, don't make us go there!" Teener spouted, "No way!" ADHD was oblivious. Driver mom moved on. But next came the help they desperately needed. A clean, pleasant-looking place to stay.
>
> Janet thanked God for the laughter that broke the spell of misery and opened the door to an evening of pleasant rest.

Can you think of moments that were traumatic at the time for you but could now be viewed as humorous?

The Bible wisely lets everyone in on a practical aid when it refers to laughter making new the heart of the hurting (Proverbs 17:22). It's an oasis offering respite. It allows patience to break through in the heart of the enduring (Proverbs 19:11; 25:15). Patience can do the same perfect work for you as you choose to make time in your life for healing, grace-enabled humor.

HEALTHY, WARM FEELINGS

Kids with special needs truly can be a barrel of laughs. Unusual joy can develop in families because of their special one. Sometimes it's not the child that brings the joy but the teamwork and support a family's network brings that initiates the healthy, warm feelings or even induces laughter into a situation. Are you able yet to experience warm feelings and laugh about some of the things that have happened to you as the parent of a child with special needs?

In the article entitled "The Happiness of Being Special" by Dawn McMullan from *Live Happy* magazine, Dawn says that "children with special needs bring much to their families: perspective, empathy and an immeasurable joy many on the outside may not see."

Therapist Carmenza Herrera Mendez has numerous beautiful memories of kids' faces and attitudes as she talked with them during therapy sessions about their lives. On one occasion, a little girl with Down syndrome asked to switch seats with her. When she did, the little girl began to refer to herself as "Carmen" and then attempted to make her therapist repeat her "pronunciation drills." Totally charming and heart warming! A time for laughter.

For Janice, the warm feelings were long in the making. She remembers the terrible twos as "terrifying twos and threes" that crept into the fours. Saving her son's life literally became a daily routine. He didn't seem to have any of the logical, healthy fears other children had. And his "creative intelligence" appeared to rarely skip a day. Some days Janice would find herself sitting and staring at the wall, lost in time from the continual stress of this child's unique activities.

One example of her son's creativity had to do with diapers. It didn't take him long to figure out that what came into the diaper from time to time was good building mortar. Another was his discovery that sharp scissors can cut through a closet full of sleeves hanging just his height! The rug wouldn't cooperate, thank God, when he found a way to set it on fire, nor did the house burn down when he decided to experiment with the excitement of being a fireman at the age of three.

Those were the days of a kind of stunned silence when Janice had no emotion. She was past all emotion. She just stood or sat staring after the necessary rescue work. Now, thirty some years later, she tells her stories and with great belly laughs, finding his creativity quite humorous even though years ago that thought was a million miles away. Prayer, time, and a new perspective made a huge difference.

SARAH'S LESSON ON LAUGHTER

In the first book of the Bible, Genesis, is a story about a couple named Abraham and Sarah. Abraham is known as the "father of faith." In the story, God comes to Abraham and promises him a son and descendants as numerous as the stars, but Sarah does not bear a son for Abraham in the normal childbearing years of the time. They wonder about that promise from God. When this couple is very elderly, the Lord comes again with the same promise. But this time, He tells them when it will happen, within the next year (Genesis 18:10–13). Sarah is far past the age of childbearing, so she laughs to herself at the thought of being a mother at her age. Abraham laughs as well.

Sarah's laugh was a laugh of doubt, but Bible commentators think Abraham's laugh was one of faith. Wouldn't you laugh too at the thought of being in your 80s or 90s and having a son? Sarah's laugh demonstrates that sometimes it only seems logical to have more faith in the way things look right now rather than what God says He can do.

Sarah had many good points, but in this instance, instead of demonstrating faith, she doubted God's promise. God heard the inward expression of her doubt even when she thought no one knew. As you read what happens next in Sarah's story, you realize that she had an extreme mind-set change.

Here's the good news. Her original doubt had no effect on the outcome! She did bear that son. In the New Testament book of Hebrews, Sarah is listed as one of the heroes of faith, as one who considered God faithful to keep His promises. Even though she doubted, God knew Sarah would come around, and the laughter of doubt would become the joy of faith. She and Abraham named their son Isaac, which means laughter (Hebrews 11:11).

TAKE TIME TO LAUGH

Take time to let laughter and rejoicing come out of your relationship with your heavenly Father and the child He has given you. Believe that your laughter and rejoicing, even in the midst of tough circumstances, will strengthen and transform your day.

Laugh because whatever is happening is laughable. Laugh at your enemies because you know God is with you. Laugh because it's chemically better for you. Laugh when you want to. Laugh because you need to. Laugh because it becomes you, and laugh because God enjoys your laughter. Laugh when there is no change, and laugh because laughter is good and life is best when you are smiling or laughing. Laugh because it's an excellent gift you don't want to miss. Laughing will change your perspective and lighten your load.

Three Close Friends

Wisdom reposes in the heart of the discerning.
(Proverbs 14:33)

Patience breaks through in the heart of the enduring.
(Proverbs 19:11; 25:15)

Laughter makes new the heart of the hurting.
(Proverbs 17:22)

Balloons

Come on, let's go, dear friends of mine.
Let's run with the new day,
giggle, have fun, and play.
You blow up the balloons.
I'll tie them with strings.
Then we'll run as if we
had wind in our wings.

The clouds have been chased away.
His love is here to stay.
God's mercy is new every morning.
See, the new day is dawning.
Let's wake the others still sleeping.
The day is ours for the keeping.

Have you ever tried to chase those clouds away by forcing laughter and just kept trying to laugh until you burst into real laughter? If you have, you realize you are hysterically funny just by trying to make yourself laugh, and it causes a natural laughter to take over. Or have you intentionally done something you were fairly certain would cause you to laugh? If not, you could try it. Some people roar with laughter when they watch old episodes of the *I Love Lucy* show. Others get a jolt of humor from a modern day sit-com or going to a website with funny animal video clips.

Finding ways to laugh is not wasted time. It's mental and physical health therapy. Even if you only have ten minutes, have something ready and waiting that you can turn to for a laugh. Laugh at what you have time for, and catch the rest later. When there's nothing within you that wants to take the time to even try smiling or laughing, do something you think might give you laughter and see what comes.

Read the advice of therapist Faith Raimer.

You CAN Celebrate!

What fun it is to celebrate. It is spirit lifting and good for the soul. Can you find reasons to celebrate? If a cause is not apparent in the moment, you may be missing the moment.

We have only to look around us for any number of seemingly small things to cheer about. Can you see the dust on the furniture and not think about the comfort of your home? Did the rain force you to cancel your plans and allow for shift of opportunity?

Look for things remarkable, things that are worthy of noticing and remarking about. Most of us have a lamp to light a room or read by, and few of us would call that remarkable unless, of course, the bulb burns out when there is no replacement supply. Electricity for our everyday use is often taken for granted (until we see the utility bill). Maybe you have a coaster with your favorite team logo, or one of those now popular electric fireplaces with multiple flame colors to suit your fancy.

The best things to celebrate are often those that cannot be purchased: a sunrise, full moon, star-lit sky, first sign of spring, and the last rose of summer. You can celebrate being an individual creation with a unique temperament, personality, and giftedness. And you can celebrate this mile of your journey. Maybe you just took a baby step that for someone else would be a giant step or vice versa. It is not about judgment. It is about accomplishment. Any baby step or boulder buster for you is worth celebrating.

Continue to look for things along your path, and you will surely find them, some obvious and some hidden as treasures fun to find. Celebrate the path unique to you and the One who made it so and gives you the light of life (John 8:12).

Laurie decided her friend needed outside help to give her a merriment boost. One day she surprised her with a quick visit and a large present. It was the Tickle Me Elmo doll. If you've never seen one, it's difficult to write how hilarious this toy can be. It's a red and furry Elmo stuffed toy based on the character

Elmo in *The Muppets* television program. When you press stuffed animal Elmo's buttons, he laughs and laughs, falls on the ground still laughing, rolls over, sits up, and keeps on laughing. Then, with a little sigh, he says, "Do it again." Few could watch this delightful, red, furry, animated laughing doll without getting tickled.

It seemed so silly to be a grown adult, with pressures on every side, taking the time to press the button and watch this doll roll, tumble, and laugh. But the quick reward was worth it all. Laurie's friend couldn't stop getting tickled at Elmo being tickled. She laughed and laughed and laughed. Then, like Elmo, she whispered, "Do it again," and pushed the button one more time.

Laughter

The laughter of Jesus rocked my soul.
Grace's favor relit perseverance's fire.
Oh patience, welcome friend,
You're bringing this trial to an end.

PRAY

Father God in heaven, forgive me for the times I've laughed, like Sarah, in doubt; and fill me with the joy of my Lord. Enable me to receive Your promises with hearty, wholesome, Abraham-style, faith-filled, thoroughly-enjoying-the-moment laughter. May I learn to smile through tears, laugh when needed in spite of sorrow, and know that real joy is rooted in an unconquerable faith in Your ultimate goodness. Help me to laugh at myself too, not taking myself too seriously. I receive Your internal joy as my personal strength. I look forward to uncovering a variety of resources that engender laughter, joy, and happiness. You think of everything! My heavenly Father, I thank you for a saving sense of humor. I love You, Lord, and am so thankful for Your gift of laughter and joy.

REFLECT

1. Consider praying these paraphrased prayers of Scripture for yourself.

    Psalm 86:4—Bring joy to your servant, for to You, O Lord, I lift up my soul.

    Psalm 97:10–11—Lord, I choose to love You and hate evil. I trust You to guard me as one of Your faithful ones. Deliver me from the hand of the wicked. I believe Your light is upon me and Your joy is in my heart. I rejoice in You, Lord, and praise Your holy name.

    John 15:13—Jesus, I will obey You by asking in Your Name so that I may receive and so that my joy may be complete, as You have told me to do.

    Jude verses 24–25—You are able to keep me from falling and to present me before Your glorious presence, without fault and with great joy. To the only God, my Savior, be glory, majesty, power, and authority, through Jesus Christ my Lord, before all ages, now and forevermore.

2. Take a moment to reflect on times that have either warmed your heart humorously or have been uproariously funny. Since science and God agree that a merry heart does "good like a medicine" (Proverbs 17:22), why not ingest some organic, effective medicine today for a heavy heart? Put off the sackcloth of mourning, and let God turn your mourning to dancing (Psalm 30:11).

3. Make a choice. Enjoy someone or something that inspires joy and laughter. Then consider reading through a few more Scriptures on joy, rejoicing, and laughter, taking note of their value.

    - Psalm 16:8–11, "I keep my eyes always on the LORD. With him at my right hand, I will not be shaken. Therefore my heart is glad and my tongue rejoices; my body also will rest secure. . . . You make known to me the path of life; you will fill me with joy in your presence, with eternal pleasures at your right hand."
    - Psalm 33:21, "In him our hearts rejoice, for we trust in his holy name."
    - Romans 14:17, "The kingdom of God is not a matter of eating and drinking, but righteousness, peace, and joy in the Holy Spirit."
    - Romans 15:13, "May the God of hope fill you with all joy and peace as you trust in him, so that you may overflow with hope by the power of the Holy Spirit."
    - Colossians 1:11, "Strengthened with all power according to his glorious might so that you may have great endurance and patience."
    - James 1:2, "Consider it pure joy, my brothers and sisters. "
    - 1 Peter 1:8–9, "Though you have not seen him, you love him; and even though you do not see him now, you believe in him and are filled with an inexpressible and glorious joy, for you are receiving the end result of your faith, the salvation of your souls."

12

Rest and Rejuvenate: Where's My Pillow?

From troubled, anxious, and restless to replenished, rejuvenated and rested

YOU'VE PROBABLY CRIED gallons of tears, stimulating those chemical hormones that relieve stress as only tears can do. It wasn't easy for your unique personality and lifestyle, but you have carved out precious respites of peace. Thank God you haven't completely lost your sense of humor and can enjoy a good belly laugh now and then. All of these activities replenish and rejuvenate, escorting in tranquil moments of much needed and deserved rest.

The night watches (or those long day watches), however, may still rattle you, causing you to crave an essential your body needs: rest. Have you ever craved your pillow? You bunch it up so it perfectly fits your face, snuggling into your favorite position. You're quietly hoping and praying you can have a full night's restful sleep. No nagging worries, repeated lists of tomorrow's must dos, or any of those other unwelcome reasons that either keep you awake or startle you from sleep. Yes, sleep, rest, ah.

There are secret mysteries hidden in your pillow time. But when your head finally hits the pillow, do you wonder for how long? Besides, you want more than just sleep for your body. You need the kind of rest that only God can provide.

THE HEART AWAKE

Susan Hafner in her booklet, *Though I Sleep, My Heart Is Awake,* says that when people sleep, their minds are at rest but their hearts are fully awake. She uses a computer analogy to say that sleep is a time when God can download into us, delete files, and defrag the confusion of our minds. "If necessary," she says, "He may even reboot our whole system."

Before we drift off to sleep, Hafner suggests that we ask God "to restore, refurbish, and refresh" us because our hearts will be awakened to receive Him. And then we can "wake up expecting God to have touched us with renewed hopes, vision, dreams, destiny, ideas, and direction."

Your spirit and soul are subject to God's Spirit and can be fully impacted by His presence bringing an infusion of His quieting nature.

Rest can come from good sleep while you are nestled on your pillow. Rest also can come from getting away from daily routine, relaxing in His presence and marinating in His promises. Rest certainly comes from personal whispering exchanges with the Savior of your soul. Learning to lean on God's sovereignty and His living truths for your life is the beginning of true rest.

The God kind of rest can reboot you like rebooting the hard drive of a computer and strengthen you like the repair of a sagging cord or ripped seam. He delights to sing gently over you like a lullaby is sung to a sleepy child. Zephaniah 3:17 reads, "The LORD your God is with you, the Mighty Warrior who saves. He will take great delight in you; in his love he will no longer rebuke you, but will rejoice over you with singing." Doesn't that verse sound absolutely soothing and dreamy, one you might turn into a prayer before your head hits the pillow? He surrounds and saturates you with Himself. His resting place is being formed within you.

RENDEZVOUS

Jesus, showing concern for His devoted followers in Mark 6:31, invites them to "come with me . . . and get some rest." Mark 6:30–31 (MSG) reads: "The apostles then rendezvoused with Jesus and reported on all that they had done and taught. Jesus said, 'Come off by yourselves; let's take a break and get a little rest.'" He knew good rest was important. Resting with Him, in His personal presence, was the point.

Another way to rest, Jesus is saying, is to get away from the crowds to a quiet place for a while, a rendezvous. It's a private place to be together. It's a meeting place with the Godhead: Father, Son, and Holy Spirit. It's a place of rest, not just a rest from routine. It's so much more. It's an infilling encounter with the all-sufficient, triune God; it's a divine interaction, an exchange of energy. It grants passage into a different view of your circumstances.

Isaiah 30:15 says, "In repentance and rest is your salvation, in quietness and trust is your strength." Matthew 11:28–29 says, "Then Jesus said, 'Come to me, all of you who are weary and carry heavy burdens, and I will give you rest. Take my yoke upon you. Let me teach you, because I am humble and gentle at heart, and you will find rest for your souls. For my yoke is easy to bear and the burden I give you is light'" (NLT).

In the original language, Greek, the words of Jesus in Mark 6:30–31 are an exclamation. Think of them as something like this: "Come and come now! I am inviting you to come!" Jesus joyfully and emphatically welcomes his disciples to come to Him, and He does so for you as well.

You are being beckoned out of routine to seek His face, which means seeking God for Himself, not just what He can do. His loving, personal presence welcomes you into His holiness. Holiness makes us, beautiful, unified, and pure. A pure heart is incredibly attractive to your heavenly Father. So seek to abide, or stick to, your Savior and Lord and Friend, Jesus Christ. There you can continually be aware of His fullness, His glorious presence dwelling in you, where all sense of negativity is superseded by your identity in Him—and that is your rest!

Come

Come to the Lamb,
Hear His calling, "Come."
The way's been made,
The price is given.
The Good Shepherd
From the dead is risen.
Join the multitude by the crystal sea.
Cry to the Lamb, "Holy.
By Your will they have their being,
Purchased with Your blood of cleansing.
Worthy are You, our Lord and our God,
Worthy are You,
Creator of all things."

A PLACE OF REST

"Heaven is My throne and earth is My footstool. Where is the house that you will build Me? Where is the place of My rest?" says Isaiah 66:1 (NKJV). In those days before the coming of Christ, God's resting place was the tabernacle. Now, however, He seeks to create in each of our hearts a sacred place for Himself, a place where He may repose with us.

For June her place of rest was a favorite wing-backed chair. Jason preferred a beach chair pushed deep in the sand at the local beach, watching the waves. For Keri it was the early hours of the morning in front of the fire in the fireplace. Few of those places offer an ongoing, daily respite free from interruption, but God has prepared a place for you every day to enter into His loving presence, experiencing "heart-to-heart transfiguration." Your place of rest—complete rest of spirit, soul, and body—is in God.

These lines by therapist Faith Raimer capture the challenge.

Who Gives Rest?

I only have to look around to see all I must do!
Then in the chaos of my day I take my eyes off You.
I chip away and try to manage passing every test,
Forgetting for the moment it is You who gives me rest.

SURROUNDED AND SATURATED

The Hebrew word in the Bible for rest is *nuach,* and it is used in many places in Scripture to mean "to rest, remain, be quiet." It also is used to indicate a "complete saturation, being surrounded" (2 Kings 2:15; Proverbs 14:33; Isaiah 11:2). Father God is looking for a relationship in which He can "completely saturate and surround" every dimension of our lives. Therein we rest.

Rest is a gift. We come to Him empty. Surrender to His gracious will. Discover our core identity. Trust His power. It's a learning and leaning process. Our Father is teaching us to rest in His strength alone. 1 Corinthians 2:5 explains why: "So that your faith might not rest on human wisdom, but on God's power." It is only by faith that we can be still, tranquil in life's circumstances. In that stillness or peacefulness, a private audience with our heavenly Father becomes a reality. We can be quieted, surrounded, and saturated simply because He IS our God. It is possible. Psalm 46:10, "Be still, and know that I am God," points us to the way.

Trust is how you "find rest for your souls" (Matthew 11:29). You trust in His working in and through you. Give yourself to the Spirit of God. Allow your heart to remain God's resting place, a holy place, where God Himself can rest. And there His love can manifest His beautifying presence, making it holy.

Love Calls

Love calls.
Holiness mates with our godly fear
Birthing obedience in our heart's desire.

PILLOW TALK

Proverbs 3:32 encourages the forgiven children of God by reminding them that it is His desire to take the upright into His confidence. The Hebrew word for *confidence* is *sode* in the original language used in Proverbs 3:32, which means pillow or cushion. It implies that God wants to take us into His "inner realm" of intimacy. Since the word is *pillow* in English, it could also mean "pillow talk," or "where God is resting." There, in that private audience, He shares His life-giving love, comfort and understanding, passions, and plans.

Confidence, inner realm, cushion, pillow talk—think of these words as descriptors of the place where God is resting and you are being invited to join Him, the Resting One.

Laura describes her pillow talks with the Lord. "It is a lot like the times my husband and I would share just before we fell asleep at night. We would be face to face, talking softly and confidentially about things we didn't talk about with other people or want overheard. I'm an outward processor. Sometimes the first time I realize what I am thinking is when I hear myself say it out loud. And then I quietly listen with a pen and paper in hand. For me it works to write what I think I am hearing.

"At first I didn't think it was a two-way conversation. But the more I practiced having these pillow talks, talking and then listening, writing and talking and then listening again, the more I began to realize I was actually in a private audience in God's presence. It didn't take long for it to dawn on me that I always felt good afterward. It became my oasis, my boost, my ever-present help in time of need. So I began intentionally carving out times, even if it was just for ten minutes."

Your Father in heaven is ready to take you into His confidence, a place of courting, His inner realm, where whisper talk takes place, into His breath space. When was your last good pillow talk, a confidential time with Him?

Therapist Michelle Phillips shares her experience with listening. "For me, usually God has to bring any change in perspective. He speaks directly to me. Later, when I share what He said, those words don't have the same impact on anyone else (although they might be helpful). When God speaks to me, I heal. I've seen it in my clients too."

God knows how to satisfy, minister, and help like no one else can. In your union with Him, you can be completely open with Him. He wants a deep, abiding interaction, friendly and loving, sharing eternal secrets. Continue your diligent yielding until His internal whispers bring a calming effect in your soul or, at the least, a whisper of the still, small voice of His Spirit's interaction.

Intentionally activate a time of holy intimacy, a pillow-talk time with your heavenly Father and Lord Jesus. It is time to let the Holy Spirit's closeness in. It will be soothing to the body, energizing to the soul, and replenishing to the mind as you enter into the rest of the Lord.

Author Susan Hafner says that your pillow, your place of rest, can be like an open window.

Open Window

God can meet us anywhere. God has a plan for you. He wants to be involved in every detail of your life. He wants to reveal to you His plans for you. He is looking for the open window of your heart to visit you. A pillow is very personal. It has your aura, your scent.

It denotes a time of intimacy. It can definitely be a regular meeting place between you and God.

Open your heart to God so He can lavish upon you the riches of His grace and love. He hears your secret longings.

Maybe it is but a desperate "911" cry of
"Help me, Lord,"
when you bury your head in your pillow
and try to fall asleep
in order to shut out
the pressures of the world.

When you lay your head on your pillow,
be assured He shows up for the meeting.
He longs for you to be there also.

Don't think for a moment you are giving God leftovers when you say bedtime prayers. It is a wonderful time to have God speak to your heart, your spirit (which is always awake) while you are at rest (finally). Never underestimate nighttime encounters with God.

Believe in faith that in your pillow time, you will be strengthened, refreshed, recharged, and supernaturally empowered by God. He will enable you to get up and out there with a fresh perspective and new energy to finish what you started.

Isaiah 66:1 says, "Heaven is my throne, and the earth is my footstool. Where is the house you will build for me? Where will my resting place be?" Turn toward your heavenly Father, your Lord Jesus, and the Holy Spirit. Take the time to lean in and trust. Rest in His love.

PRAY

Dear Lord Jesus, open my eyes that I may see. Open my ears that I may hear what the Holy Spirit is revealing about true rest and how we can commune in quiet times as well as when I am sleeping. I trust my weakness is immersed in Your grace. I believe my confidence is growing as I keep looking to You and what You are bringing into my inner most being. I trust You to restore, refurbish, and refresh me. Thank you for quieting me by Your love and rejoicing over me with singing.

REFLECT

1. Your heavenly Father has given you an open-ended invitation to a rendezvous—to meet with Him. When you opened the door of your heart, He entered. Now His personal presence is readily available! What about seeking God encounters while you intentionally rest? Would a few minutes listening to music or quietly sitting in a comfortable chair be a good way to rest and rendezvous? How about hiking in the early morning or a neighborhood stroll in the afternoon? Wherever or whenever you choose, expect God to be with you.

2. As Susan Hafner suggested, don't underestimate your nighttime encounters with the Lord. Just before you put your head on your favorite pillow to sleep, consider taking a moment to write down one request. Ask Him boldly for a rendezvous, believing for knowledge, revelation, and an internal transformation encounter!

13

Trials, Triumphs & Connections: Can Miracles Happen?

From alone, out ranked, and ill-equipped to gutsy teamwork and perseverant transfiguration

Miracles come in many forms. Happenstance or God initiated? Just hard work driven? In biblical Greek, the word *miracle* means "by might or power, or marvelous works; power through God's ability." By definition, if an event is not ascribable to human power or the laws of nature, it's attributed to a supernatural, divine agency or God working through the laws of nature.

A miracle is beyond anything that can be worked out or fully explainable. "If you see a turtle resting on a fence post," said one southern gentleman, "you know it didn't get there by itself." It is definitely beyond, way beyond the achievable.

Parenting a child with special needs launched you into the miracle realm. Your first and deepest desire was probably for the miracles that would eliminate the most pressing needs. Reading through the Bible, who can deny that possibility? And yet, miracles can take many different forms.

SEPARATING

Having moved mostly through the first three stages of transformation as the parent of a child with special needs—*surviving, searching, settling*—it's only natural to consider what the *separating* stage will be like.

Separating is the last stage of what truly has been a journey filled with many small miracles. As you look back over all you have experienced so far, are you able to discern any noticeable miracles that have transpired? What miracles can you foresee or wish for ahead?

SEEING MIRACLES

Years ago I saw a cover of a nature magazine that displayed a sketch of a large pelican that had just scooped up a frog with its broad and deep bill. The frog's long, thin arms were hanging out of each side of the bill. Those frail frog arms were squeezing the pelican's neck with all their might.

It was obvious in the sketch that the skinny little frog was determined to force open the pelican's large bill and hop out. Or maybe it could strangle that pelican in order to get free. One way or another, the scrawny frog was determined to get out of its predicament. The caption below the artist's rendition of the frog's perseverance read, "It's not over until it's over." Can you relate?

I Feel Like a Grasshopper in a Bird's Nest (or a Frog in the Pelican's Bill)!

Have you ever felt helpless,
victimized,
or little more than a vulnerable grasshopper
in your search for medical, emotional,
physical, financial, or educational help for your child?

This poem's message is not an uncommon complaint. During the months, sometimes years of searching for the right doctor, service, medication, or other needs, parents often run into insensitive, uninformed people who speak or act without any or little understanding. What is the best for your child? Do the authorities really know?

It could be you're not sure you know. In the middle of the searching, it is only logical at times to feel very intimidated. After all, there seem to be unending reasons for learning what works best. Educated authority figures in particular can seem very threatening. Handling the occasional harsh or cold responses can be infuriating. Therapist Faith Raimer describes one of those times for her.

> As I look back on my time working with kids who faced incredible odds of making it in a world we can move freely about in and sometimes take for granted, I am reminded what an unmistakable blessing God gave me. At times the therapy work seemed endless and worse, fruitless.
>
> I wish I could say that every one of those kids I saw left my care changed for the better and continued that way. I can't. But I can say I was given an amazing opportunity to see them, by God's grace, through the eyes of my heart and able to honor them in that parenthesis of time. It is my hope that as I looked for the good in them, they were better able to find it in themselves.
>
> Romans 14:19 says, "So let us then definitely aim for and eagerly pursue what makes for harmony and for mutual upbuilding (edification and development) of one another" (AMP). You can remind any child AND yourself: when you feel you're just a little cog, your Father is a BIG WHEEL! You are a COG, a child of God, and that makes you an important part of the wheel.

Numerous parents and caregivers can testify of having no explanation for what happened next after they came face to face with what seemed like indifference or hopelessness. Nevertheless, they tell of miracles that happened in their children; in their experiences with family, friends, and local and trans-local systems; and even in organizations. But most of all, the miracles they testify of experiencing were *in themselves.* In it all, through it all, they were personally transformed!

Perseverance

Often when perseverance finds a way,
And then looks back upon its path,
It discovers, lo and behold,
It was not chance when it took its stance,
But the way was appointed from of old.

WATER INTO WINE

The book of John, chapter 2, tells a story about Jesus and His mother attending a wedding in Cana. In the culture of the day, wine was expected at wedding feasts. Being without abundant wine was an insult to the guests. On this occasion, the wine ran out, so Mary petitioned her son for help. She knew He could help.

At first it appeared Jesus would do nothing. It wasn't His time to reveal His full identity. And yet, because the friends hosting the wedding celebration had a need and His mother asked for His help, Jesus told the servants to go and fill the large water jars with fresh water. After filling the jars, the servants took them to the wine steward. He tasted the contents. Shock! The water had not only been transformed to wine, but it tasted like the best of the best, equal to what he thought was the king's finest wine!

Confusion set in when others tasted it too. Why, when the guests were already tipsy and couldn't tell the difference between cheap and expensive wine, would the hosts serve such quality? Why had they saved the best for last? It was a mystery for most. Only Jesus and the servants who knew that water had been changed to wine at the command of Jesus grasped the miracle. To all others it was wine, just more wine. Yes, it was the best, and yet none could tell that there was anything supernatural about the wine.

In this story Jesus took the natural and turned it into another form of nature—the best of the best that could be offered—and He did it with servants who followed His instructions. They saw the miracle. They experienced the supernatural when others just saw it as one more glass of ordinary wine.

Water to Wine

Jesus changed the water at Cana, in Galilee,
to reveal His power, thus transforming me
into His likeness,
into His likeness.

Born of water,
born of Spirit,
the water made wine,
His best is now mine.

Jesus changed the water at Cana, in Galilee,
revealing His miraculous ability.
Born of water,
born of Spirit,
into faith
I was thrust.
In His workmanship,
I now trust.

Only servants saw the water change.
Only the one born again
can see God's Kingdom reign.
Jesus, my Lord, all has become new
since I've learned to draw from You.

God's love was changed into the blood of Jesus.
By the gift of grace,
resurrection power has released us.
Born of the Spirit,
I've entered into the blood-bought exchange.
Now bone of Your mercy
and flesh of Your grace,
I remain.

Water and Spirit agree.
Wed with Your Word in
favor and sweet unity.
You saved the best till last.
Love's excellence fulfilled!
What more could I ask
as to Your mercy I yield?

Jesus revealed His glory
in this little gospel story.
He turned the water to wine,
declaring God's best would be mine.

SIGNS AND WONDERS

God confirmed Jesus through mighty works, wonders, and signs (Acts 2:22). God confirmed His words with the signs that followed in Mark 16:20, and the

Lord bore witness to His word with signs and wonders (Acts 14:3). Signs, miracles, and wonders are consistently recorded throughout the New Testament by Jesus and by His followers (Acts 2:43; 2 Corinthians 12:12; Romans 15:9).

Paul and Barnabas recounted the signs and wonders God had done through them (Acts 15:12). Jesus' followers prayed that God would continue to grant signs and wonders in the name of Jesus (Acts 4:30). Steven performed great wonders and signs (Acts 6:8). People recorded seeing Philip perform signs (Acts 8:6).

There are a multitude of references to signs, miracles, and wonders in the Bible. They can and do happen in our times as well. Read Ron and Cassie's story of what they saw as miraculous.

Our Miracle

It all started when we noticed that our 4-month-old baby daughter, Cassie, didn't notice or track the movement of the hanging crib toys. She did turn her head to sounds, though. Not knowing the extent of the issue and gulping even at the thought of her having to wear glasses as a toddler, we thought it best to have her examined.

The test showed that Cassie was experiencing little, if any, light perception from her retina. Her eyes had a deficit of rods and cones, and the doctor described the condition of her eyes as being like a working camera but without film. Our daughter was blind.

There were what seemed at the time to be small miracles as she grew, but in retrospect, the real miracles were in the success of our advocacy for her. We were able to get Cassie to mainstream in the public school system and university at a time when the expertise and specialists for special needs kids was just beginning to make appearances.

Some would consider our victories as nothing miraculous, but we knew God had worked a wonder for our daughter. Cassie graduated from college and is a successful woman. We were also able to meet and encourage other special needs families along the way and pioneer the use of new technologies that were just appearing and maturing in the 80s and 90s.

Miraculous changes have happened for others as well. For Gregory, his ADHD and dyslexia were a constant struggle. He was thirteen when he was prayed over specifically for his condition, and his parents noticed an immediate difference. The symptoms seemed to just disappear! His parents were friends with a family whose young girl had similar symptoms, so they shared what had happened to their son. The young girl came for prayer, and as he prayed for her, she too was miraculously delivered!

Justin was in another country, sharing the love of Jesus, when a mom came up to this young man and asked for prayer for her very young child who had never walked. Justin had never seen a miracle let alone prayed for someone who experienced a miracle from God. But in that hour, the child not only stood but also walked. It was so shocking to everyone that his mother even fainted!

Vanessa fell while she was roller-skating. The protrusion under the skin looked like a small bone break and was very painful. As she and her mother prayed, they could actually see the movement under the skin, and the pain left her ankle! Surprised and not sure how to respond, they were overwhelmed with the miracle. Thank you, thank you, thank you is all they could think to say.

Cheryl was praying for several people when she heard an announcement that miracles were happening in her part of the room. She looked up, wondering where they were, and realized the announcement was about the people she had just prayed for! What? They could hear? The moment itself is a mystery, a sign, and a wonder because Cheryl herself still wore a hearing aid.

IT'S IN THE DEFINITION

Margaret and John missed it for years. Only much later would they see the miracles.

> Looking back, we ask ourselves why we didn't see the miracles and wonders that we now readily share with others. We believe it was because we had one focus, the eradication of the problem. Nothing else

> could possibly be a sign or miracle or cause a sense of awe and wonder unless the situation itself disappeared. Once we settled our hearts on the fact that God is good and heaven is a real place, the glories of His grace were more readily seen.
>
> Our daughter left us from a brain tumor younger than we hoped and prayed. But get this! Before she went home to be with our Lord, she believed in miracles and would pray for others. We saw God heal and deliver people as she prayed for them in a moment of time. It was undeniable and miraculous. We took it as a sign that her need would soon disappear. But it didn't. Her time with us was years longer than doctors said possible, and for this we are thankful.
>
> In her last sentences, she spoke of believing she would minister to the world of God's love. Only God knows how true her desire was and its impact for eternity.

Jason's story was shared earlier in this book, but the ending perspective his mother shared was saved for this later chapter. Read how one child of special needs fulfilled a special purpose that would impact lives for many years to come.

Jason's Getaway

> Jason, like all of us, desired to make a difference in the world with his life. His desire was fulfilled through his interaction with an important person in his life, his caregiver, Debbie.
>
> Debbie is a special needs teacher who gives her heart to every child. She has been Jason's respite provider since he was a small child. For many years she has had a desire to have a place for special needs children, parents, and individuals in group homes to go. A place that is not too expensive but fun and relaxing and ultimately a learning experience. For two years, Debbie prayed about her desire, but nothing came about: no direction, no nothing.
>
> One day she was helping Jason get dressed and they were singing their usual songs to lessen the anxiety of transition. He was singing his

favorite song, "Old McDonald Had a Farm," when Debbie had an epiphany. She just knew that the place she was prayerfully seeking should be a farm where people could experience animals and learn about farm life while they are having fun.

Her insight that day propelled her forward in getting it started, and in honor of my son, she named it Jason's Getaway. The Facebook page for the place is up, but the funds have not yet been fully raised to open it.

"I am a miracle. Jason is a miracle," says Debbie. "We live in a relationship with a miraculously, loving, faithful God through His Son Jesus Christ by the guide and power of the Holy Spirit."

Jason's Getaway is a sign, a miracle, and a wonder!

PRAY

Jesus, Lord and our Redeemer, who was and is and is to come:

It's incredible You refer to me as Your friend. You've said that others would know You by our love. It goes beyond understanding's height, width, depth, or length to realize that I have been called a friend of the Author of creation and Finisher of my faith! I surrender the future into Your loving wisdom for whatever comes, whether a sign, a miracle, or a wonder. I await the potential of them all. At the same time, I trust Your eternal purposes and choose to be a miracle of Your love, a sign to those around me as they wonder how I can be at rest.

Whether I ever see a miraculous change or not, may the impossible become possible in me. Again I pray, until I see You face to face or in the answer that I seek, I believe I shall be found in Your abiding grace, my soul quieted by Your peace.

REFLECT

1. You may not have experienced a full restoration miracle, but you long to know that His presence has initiated a sign, miracle, or wonder in your family. What stirs inside of you as you read the words of Psalm 31:24, "Be strong and take heart all you who hope in the Lord"?

2. What miracles, signs, or wonders can you share with others based on the words of John 14:27, "Peace I leave with you; my peace I give you. I do not give to you as the world gives. Do not let your hearts be troubled and do not be afraid"?

3. This is your opportunity for a victory lap of honor. Victory laps are run by the winning person or team to celebrate a victory. How have you been comforted that now you can run a victory lap by comforting others, celebrating what God has brought you through? Consider saying a prayer for those individuals today even though you may not know their names or circumstances. "Praise be to the God and Father of our Lord Jesus Christ, the Father of compassion and the God of all comfort, who comforts us in all our troubles, so that we can comfort those in any trouble with the comfort we ourselves receive from God" (2 Corinthians 1:3–4).

14

Finite Infinity—Limited Yet Unlimited!

From diagnosed lack and limitations to creative, eternal, unlimited potential

ONE VERY SPECIAL evening, Doug shared with his group a picture his son, Peter, had drawn. Peter's disease caused him to spend most of his day in a wheelchair, so he enjoyed passing the time by drawing. The picture Doug shared was a well-drawn likeness of a kiwi bird. Below it, Peter had written, "God loves you even if you can't fly!"

Young Peter had found a likeness between him and the kiwi bird. But even more significant was his far-beyond-his-years revelation of God's love. He understood that God loves each of His children regardless of their abilities.

KIWIS

Kiwis, birds indigenous to New Zealand, have no tail and tiny 2-inch wings, which for all practical purposes are useless. Even though they have wings, the bones in their chests do not have the capacity for flight muscles, which is what a bird also needs to fly. Despite their awkward appearance, kiwis have abilities other birds do not. They can actually outrun a human. They survive because of their keen alertness and sharp, 3-toed feet, which enable them to kick and slash an enemy.

Is the comparison too obvious? Maybe your precious one can't "fly" through a public school class or homework as other children. He or she may not be able to fly in socially acceptable behaviors or return the love and affection you pour over him or her. Maybe your child can't fly down the street at a running pace or even make it through one day without getting someone upset. Still, in his or her own way, your child can fly.

What do you think about when you see moms and dads who appear to be super heroes in the latest movie compared to you? Somehow they seem to manage more responsibility in a day than you do, and to top it off, they seem to do so with a greater ease. Their accomplishments can make you feel more tired than you already are just thinking about it. You might wonder, *Where are my wings?*

As you sift and sort through the myriad of decisions you make each day, try to remember how much God loves you and your children right now just as you are. His love is not just a deeply sincere, emotional feeling. It's practical. It's empowering. It's everlasting. You have inherent, God-like spiritual DNA—God's family traits. You and your child are valuable to Him. You are His very own, even if no one in the family "flies just like the other birds."

ASTRO BLASTER CAPABILITIES

Have you seen the movie *Buzz Lightyear?* The main character, Buzz, is a Disney cartoon toy person dressed in a white space suit. When the button on the front of his suit is pushed, wings appear. Just before he takes off in flight, he shouts, "To infinity and beyond!"

Disneyland's Buzz Lightyear Astro Blasters ride makes sure everyone knows Buzz has Astro blaster capabilities. The loudspeaker blaring the message sets the stage for the ride. Park goers are invited to join Buzz by enlisting in a space fighting force to destroy the enemy's plan. The parallels to God and His powerful resources available to you as the parent of a child with special needs appear in brackets within the ride experience description here.

> First, Buzz Lightyear and the Galactic Alliance appeal to the wide-eyed riders for help by climbing aboard the interactive ride to blast enemy targets and save an imaginary galaxy with the familiar phrase, "To infinity and beyond!"
>
> The riders agree to enlist with the Star Command [*God and His angels*] as a Space Ranger [*committed believer*] to join his brigade [*body of Christ*]. What is their noble goal? To destroy the enemy! They will destroy Zurg's army and thwart his evil plan: to steal the batteries [*the power source*] from good toys everywhere so Zurg can fuel his Ultimate Secret Weapon [*death*]!
>
> In the briefing room [*prayer room*], riders see the secret map of the Galactic Alliance and have a personal encounter with Buzz Lightyear himself (*the Holy Spirit*). Buzz lets them in on the adventure of a lifetime just ahead for them: to join him in saving the Little Green Men and defeating Zurg's evil robots, who are stealing the batteries.
>
> Next comes the training. Riders learn how to use their Astro blaster [*skill and spiritual awareness*], a toy space gun with an optically safe laser beam. When all are safely buckled in, the ride rolls and shakes, the loud clashing of battle sounds in every ear, and the enemy is defeated. Peace has returned to the planet!

"Infinity and beyond" in God's eternal Kingdom is your future and your family's future forevermore. In other words, finite humans who have given their lives to Jesus have infinite possibilities for a victorious life. They have a guarantee for their lives that goes beyond this earth and into infinity—from limited to unlimited. They can blast past boundaries into the unknown with Jesus Christ as Commander.

Keeping this eternal perspective in focus can help you adapt to your child's lack of wings and, at the same time, help you remain watchful for those special, surprise gifts and abilities.

ABILITIES AND DISABILITIES

Have you read those stories of children with autism who graduate from college? True, not every child with autism is a savant beneath the surface. But when a parent steps into the treasure hunt for hidden abilities behind a child's visible or hidden special needs, there's typically more there than what meets the eye.

The story of what happened in the life of an Indiana child with autism and an IQ of 170 is not unique. Every school setting his parents tried to place him in defined him as "unfit for a regular classroom." The situation didn't look good, but his mother kept searching for creative ways to place him in a learning environment to unlock what she knew to be true about his intellect.

Startled one day by his ability to repeat complicated sets of information about star formations, the child's mother began to explore more expansive ways to free him to be all he could be. Specialists continued to classify him and his abilities incorrectly while his mother intentionally gave him chances to learn and grow and thrive. In time his diagnosis was changed from severely limited to unlimited. His capabilities are such that experts say he has the potential of winning the famed Nobel Prize in physics.

Who knew? Only God and this diligent parent! And what might this child's eternal assignment be? Only God knows that one. It's a mystery. Likewise, the parents of this gifted child and parents of children with special needs have a myriad of fascinating mysteries to unravel as their children grow.

Mystery is a word that intrigues and yet frightens. How a television works is a mystery to many; nevertheless they use it liberally. Even though the details of how computers function are mysterious to most people, they spend hours each day making use of all computers have to offer.

FROM FINITE TO INFINITE

What will your assignment and your child's be when you cross the threshold from earth to heaven, from finite to infinity? It is one of those glorious mysteries, beyond your limited dreaming capacity. Eternal mysteries are not intended by God to be frightening. Instead, they can elevate and exhilarate the imagination. Wow! Life without limitation!

Living in God's realm (another word is *Kingdom*, the place where He reigns) means there is a continual invitation for you to explore more of Him and what His abilities mean in your persona and purpose. His realm is a "now" realm, not just a "some day" one. The creative, empowering, majestic Spirit of God is alive in you, so why not expect to go beyond your limitations!

His fullness is being revealed in your everyday existence. God's goodness is without measure. You and your child can have a significant impact on those around you. You are conduits of hope and instruments that carry what others need of His grace, goodness, glory, and multiplied peace.

The Creator gave us a natural mind to deal with natural things. He gave us a finite mind to deal with the finite world. He also fashioned us with an infinite spirit to relate to His infinite nature. We can't take an infinite God and fit Him into a finite mind, but our spirit can grasp His infinite Spirit.

The expression "the sky is the limit" is a truth we can hold onto, defeating the "ants at our picnic" and any "threatening giants." The Word of God, the Bible, becomes Spirit and life to our whole being as we spend time absorbing the powerful truths that lie within it. The Word speaks to our spirit, and with these truths He lifts our limits.

Bill's mother, Denette, watched as her son struggled to keep up with the other boys his age. One day his mother took him aside to encourage him with an eternal perspective. "Bill some day you will be able to walk and run just like the other boys." With an absolute certainty in his voice, Bill responded, "Mom, I'm not going to just run. I'm going to fly!"

GOD'S VERY BEST

Each of Nancy Miller's stages of transformational parenting has its challenges, but the *separating stage* is unique for each family. The separating stage encompasses events as diverse as letting a child go out on the patio without holding a hand to a child's departure from earth and entrance into the heavenly realm.

Usually when it is time to let go on some level, thoughts such as *I haven't had enough time to prepare my child adequately* bombard the mind. *Have I done all I could?* and *It just feels too early* are typical responses. And, of course, when it's time to release a child into the arms of Jesus, how could the timing ever seem right?

Grandma Carol Martin shared the story of separation in her son's family.

God's Very Best

> My grandson, Ryan, was diagnosed at age three with autism. At age fourteen, he was placed in a group home operated by his state, living life as a low functioning autistic child. The home is located about three hours from his family.
>
> Things in the family home had come to a boiling point, with danger to family and others. Ryan's anxiety and frustrations had been coming out in hitting, hard pinching, and repetitive, obsessive actions with no sense of boundaries. For years Ryan had taken strong anti-psychotic, anti-anxiety medications to moderate his behaviors and reactions. Attempts to take him off meds came with even more severe negative behaviors. In my son's words, his family was "tapped out" and had no more to give.
>
> For me, seeing Ryan go outside the family home to live was a heart wrenching and sad situation, even though it was a necessary decision. For his immediate family, the decision to place Ryan in a group home came with anxiety yet a sense of relief, their "hearts arguing with their minds" in the days leading up to his placement. A dear friend prayed for me over this situation. Her prayer was for "nothing but God's very best for your son's family."
>
> After fourteen years filled with fears, unexpected experiences, and endless emotions and tears, God's "very best" was happening for Ryan and his family. Ryan was in a safe home with caregivers who were qualified and had the energy, patience, care, and wisdom to reach him and teach him and meet his various needs. A year earlier, such a possibility was not even on the radar, and the entire family was sinking lower and lower under the weight of the challenges of caring for Ryan in the home. God was beginning the healing and restoration needed in all their lives.

The weekend after Ryan's placement, the family went to visit Ryan for the first time since he'd left home. They had a good lunch together with lots of hugs and love, and that is how it should be for a family. The group home staff contacted the parents later to report that Ryan did very well the week after the visit, and that the family visit was really a good thing for him. This call was truly a report of the Lord, which encouraged his parents. They began looking forward to arrangements they'd made to have him home for three days at the upcoming holiday break.

I thank God for bringing Ryan, his family, and all of us through this hard season of life. We have passed through to the other side, and I believe there is hope, healing, and a bright future ahead for the entire family!

Worth It?

There are beautiful blossoms that seem to defy the season's call.
There are seasons for blooming so short one marvels
why the blossoms bother to bloom at all.
A common sense business evaluation would ask, "Will it be worth it?"
A logical response would be to acknowledge, "Not unless I make a good profit!"
If you made the choice to plant, water, and cultivate,
how much would be enough benefit
before you considered the work worth the wait?

Arctic Seasons

In the Arctic the flowers seem to cram three seasons into one.
Does it matter how long until their blooms are undone?
The deep reds, lavish purples, and sun-gold yellows
share the flowering overtures.
In the brevity of the visit, each reveals priceless treasures.

HOW LONG IS ENOUGH?

Elaine's story about separation may offer treasures of insights for what might be ahead for you.

As Easy as Falling Asleep

Separating stages reoccur until there is no more separation possible. Knowing that Matt could live only to his early teens was really tough to handle. This is what the doctors told us when they first diagnosed him at age four and a half. In response, I chose to stay at home and care for him. With the help of technology and Matt's own will to live, he was able to live many more years.

Once Matt graduated from high school and went to one year of junior college, he pretty much hung out with me at home. When he was around twenty-one years old, it seemed to me he was getting weaker and weaker. Once he had to go to the hospital with an upper respiratory infection, and he got a small bed sore from the hospital that took almost ten months to clear up.

I would try to talk to Matt about heaven and what it would be like. I would share what my husband and I knew to be true in Scriptures. Verses such as 2 Corinthians 5:8, "We are confident, I say, and would prefer to be away from the body and at home with the Lord," were a comfort. I wanted him to be prepared, and I wanted to be prepared too.

I needed at least four caregivers to help me care for Matt. At one point Matthew could only be in his wheelchair for no more then three hours at one time. Finally it became necessary to put Matt in hospice, not really knowing how much longer he would live. As it turned out, he was in hospice care for two and a half years. I was always afraid the insurance company would tell me he was in hospice for too long, but thankfully that never happened.

During the hospice years, I was writing in my journal, praying to God, and asking Him why Matt hadn't received a physical healing

> because I believe God is the healer and I had prayed for Matt's healing for over twenty years. I remember so clearly when God shared with me that His concern was more about the inward heart than the physical. Believe it or not, this truth set me free.
>
> I realized Matt had a God calling on his life. He loved the Lord and would share Christ with all his caregivers. He couldn't turn the pages of his Bible, so the caregivers would listen to him while he read out loud and turn the pages for him. When it became too difficult for him to read, they would read to him. I knew that Matt's heart was one with God. From that day forward, I knew that Matt was accomplishing what God had called him to do. He was a preacher of the Good News of God's love with those lovely ladies who took care of him.
>
> My motto was then and still is today is to *live each day with no regrets*! It does no good to play the I-wish-I-would-have, the I-could-have, or the I-should-have mind game. My goal was that when Matt went home to be with the Lord, he would not have a bedsore or be sick with a cold or the flu.
>
> Our miracle came true. Matt was watching one of his movies and just fell asleep very peacefully.

There's a fairly well-known story these days about what heaven might be like for all children and also those who have trusted Christ as Savior and Lord before their transitioning into eternal life. In the book *Heaven is for Real: A Little Boy's Astounding Story of His Trip to Heaven and Back* by Todd Burpo, a story unfolds of a young boy whose appendix burst. During his time in the hospital, he has an encounter with Jesus and heaven. As the parents begin to realize their son has had something amazing occur, they slowly ask simple questions, patiently waiting for his astounding story to be revealed. It emerges with a child's simplicity. For example, when asked whether he saw people walking or flying in heaven, the boy's simple answer is that there in heaven everyone flew.

The young boy's encounters in heaven bear a strong likeness to God's revealed heart and description of heaven in the Bible. They are filled with real people talking and enjoying each other. What a wonderful encouragement to read the stories in this book that elaborate the Bible's description of reality. The fact that heaven is real and the truth that we have relatives living there are foundational to our sense of continuing forevermore.

When those you love enter this loving, glorious realm, it helps to know one day you will see them again. But their passing is still a tremendous loss for each earthbound one. "Do not let your hearts be troubled. You believe in God; believe also in me. My Father's house has many rooms; if that were not so, would I have told you that I am going there to prepare a place for you?" Jesus said on His last night on earth with the disciples (John 14:1–2). His going means He has prepared an eternal and wonderful place customized just for you also. What is implied but not spelled out is that the Holy Spirit comes into your life here on earth to make you into the house that matches your eternal habitation. He moves into you, and then one day He moves you home.

Emily Zimbrich experienced a God intervention in her separating grief at the loss of her husband.

> One week before our thirty-sixth wedding anniversary, my life was forever changed. My husband, Gene, suddenly passed away in his sleep. As the days and months passed, the grief seemed at times unbearable until one snowy day about six months later as I was listening to a CD by Graham Cooke and cleaning. I remember standing at the bathroom sink when I heard him say, "The time for grieving is over."
>
> I looked up and felt the deep-seated grief physically leave my body like a whoosh. It was a miracle. After that day, I felt lighter, had more energy, and the crying stopped. Today, almost five years later, I still miss him and wish he were here; however, the heaviness that left that day is gone.

As you prepare for the separation stage in your life and the life of others you love, know that you are being invited into a superior reality. It's not imagination. It's not just positive thinking. It is the reality of everlasting, supernatural life in Christ Jesus your Lord, Savior, and forever friend.

Kiwis

Kiwi birds can't fly!
Do even experts know why?
Every part seems to be there,
Yet they cannot fly in the air.
What happened in the womb?
What slowed down?
What sped up too fast?
What made that piece
Fall from the lap?
What can be done?
Who holds the clue?
Is it me?
Is it him?
Is it you?
Does every bird have to fly?
Does every person have to be like you or I?

OTHER WINGS

Should this blip of life here and now be allowed to be the only determining factor of your identity and destiny?

The Author of Life invites you into the God life to be satisfied in Him, both now and forever. God's adventure of separation is not boring but glorious. You can experience His multi-faceted and eternal nature—filled with His goodness, nothing dark, foreboding, or ugly in it. Brilliant beauty internally and externally will fill your whole being with inestimable majestic love.

As you take off on this "adventure ride," you will experience amazing and wonderful things He has planned from long ago. Then, when it's time for you or those you love to step off this earth, transitioning to heaven's realm will be a glorious new beginning for all Jesus' family. You can rejoice that in Him you have everlasting life and that you will again be united with those who have gone on before you.

Philippians 3:20 says, "But our citizenship is in heaven. And we eagerly await a Savior from there, the Lord Jesus Christ." Acts 1:11 says, "This same Jesus, who has been taken from you into heaven, will come back in the same way you have seen him go into heaven."

No matter what doesn't come to pass here and now, you and your child are God's prize, and He has prepared a place for you. He makes the difference in your reality today and into your eternal reality as you continue to look to Him for the fullness of identity, forgiveness, strength, wisdom, and eternal purpose—to infinity and beyond!

It's important to realize that infinity began the day you were conceived. As a believer in Jesus Christ, the Son of God, your eternal residence was determined the day you were "born from above" as a citizen of heaven. It's a given. You will fly. You are children of finite infinity. A thrilling adventure awaits.

BEYOND

Psalm 8:1–4 (MSG) reads, "GOD, brilliant Lord, yours is a household name. Nursing infants gurgle choruses about you; toddlers shout the songs that drown out enemy talk, and silence atheist babble. I look up at your macro-skies, dark and enormous, your handmade-sky-jewelry, Moon and stars mounted in their settings. Then I look at my micro-self and wonder, Why do you bother with us? Why take a second look our way?"

After reading this passage, your first thought is probably the same as many others. "Why take a second look our way?" That's an excellent question. What does God, the creator of heaven and earth, see of great value in humankind? The answer is His likeness, His family, and your personal destiny.

The God life is forever. We will see loved ones again in the next round of life. We will experience what it means to have an infinite destiny; an elaborate, beyond-your-imagination extension of the original spiritual purpose and talents

God designed in each of us. Earth existence may be finite, but spiritual life is infinite.

God's love challenges and stuns our imagination. His desire to embrace us as His family extends our reason to marvel. He is letting us in on an incredible secret. Life eternal begins now, not just when we die. Now we can embrace infinity by progressively getting to know the true God and His Son Jesus Christ (John 3:15–16; 6:40; 17:3). The Bible is definite about the fact that one day each of us will have a new glorified body (1 Corinthians 15:44). Our curiosity can't help but wonder what it's going to be like.

Read the account of Jesus after His resurrection. His followers recognized Him. He talked like Jesus, and He ate and enjoyed the company of His friends. Of course, there were some remarkable changes. He could walk through walls, appeared at will, and moved from earth to heaven like one ascending into the clouds.

Jesus made it clear, by showing up after His death and burial and clothed in His new glorious spiritual body, talking, eating, and teaching, that life extends beyond the grave. Todd Burpo's story in the book, Heaven Is for Real, is just one of several books talking about the glorious realities of life after leaving this earth. Young Todd experienced recognizing loved ones in heaven and having a new, perfect body for infinity—one that can fly! Likewise, all who believe in Him will fly beyond anything they could ask for or dream of!

Heavenly life, as these stories and descriptions reveal, isn't an ethereal, formless, vague existence of personhood where spirits become one or float around. Instead, life at its finest is catapulted into jubilant ecstasy with divine intention and purpose. Heaven is a real place with tangible homes and recognizable people overtaken by indescribable joy. Since that's a Christian's miraculous destiny, when can anyone actually claim that life is ever really "over"?

So keep on keeping on, having done all to stand, and with confidence as Ephesians 6:13–14 encourages, which is until earth's boundaries explode into heaven's eternal, boundless wonder. Continue in all you know as revealed to you by your Maker, and as the Lord spoke to my heart: "Until I see You face to face, or in the answer that I seek, may I be found in Your abiding grace, my soul quieted by Your peace!"

Remember these words from "Buttercups Under Ice."

You must remember life extends beyond this hour.
Trust God's loving care and willingness to empower.

For those who have eyes to see, even nature preaches a hopeful tale.
And what is her good news?
There's reason for hope beyond each dark veil.

Keeping a healthy, God-born perspective soothes the aching soul and keeps the eyes open to see His handiwork, both in the tiny, incremental shifts and the drastic, creative, supernatural provisions.

PRAY

Jesus, I thank You. You have swallowed up death in victory. You are the resurrection and the life! Heaven is a real place. Life extends beyond this hour and forever— miraculously glorious, beautiful, and filled beyond my ability to imagine with resurrection life.

Infinity is a word that shortens the breath, so it's no surprise to You that these truths seem out of my grasp. But thanks be unto You, my heavenly Father, that in and by Your creative majesty, You've found a way to give me a sense of knowing that supersedes all that reasoning might say. Help me believe, receive, and perceive Your signs, miracles, and wonders. I am grateful indeed for Your eternal greatness that lifts me beyond the limitations of mere humanity!

REFLECT

1. Does identity and value depend on the quantity and quality of the ruling sphere of influence that one experiences during life here on earth alone? Length of stay? Abilities compared to others? How does your answer to this question challenge your perspective of what is valuable?

2. Who do you know or have heard about whose gifts, talents, personality, and purpose unfolded in the midst of their special needs that were even more profound than anyone could have fathomed?

3. Read 1 Corinthians 12:21–26 and think about your child's abilities and special needs.

   > The eye cannot say to the hand, "I don't need you!" And the head cannot say to the feet, "I don't need you!" On the contrary, those parts of the body that seem to be weaker are indispensable, and the parts that we think are less honorable we

> treat with special honor. And the parts that are unpresentable are treated with special modesty, while our presentable parts need no special treatment. But God has put the body together, giving greater honor to the parts that lacked it, so that there should be no division in the body, but that its parts should have equal concern for each other. If one part suffers, every part suffers with it; if one part is honored, every part rejoices with it.

4. Your "kiwi bird" may not be able to fly like other birds, but in what ways does your child soar? How does your kiwi bird fly?

Epilogue

A Trumpet Call of Prophetic Words

THE WRITING OF this book has been an incredible journey of faith and struggle. It was conceived many years ago, and the labor of bringing it forth has been long and complex. In every step and misstep along the way, however, the hand of the Lord has been in mine. He has led my feet to the ground on which I stand today and offer these words of hope and encouragement to you.

Thanks be unto God, the Christian life is more than just learning how to be obedient to a set of standards. Our Lord Jesus encourages us with hope and divine purpose. Breathtaking revelations of His marvelous nature intended for the expanse of the whole created universe are ours to enjoy. He begins by first giving us a small taste. He grants us responsibility and managing opportunity in our families and homes and then communities, states, and even in nations—everywhere our sphere of influence can make a difference. His eternal purpose is to extend our influence throughout the universe. His plan is a unified transformation that is meant to be infinite and everlasting.

Your disappointments and challenges are the boot camp for privileged special ops training. You are becoming the peace that surpasses understanding. You are being qualified to impart wisdom and courage.

God didn't initiate the negative, challenging traits or difficult circumstances your child with special needs brought into your life. The circumstances themselves have caused you to be a chosen one within them. Your willingness to continually look to Him while parenting your child with special needs has become your qualifier. You have become the chosen of God for a specialized training, culminating in His glorious, eternal purposes and your everlasting destiny.

Special operations training is yours in Christ Jesus. You will make a significant impact. You are in the company of multitudes of parents with similar potential. Through it all you are being equipped to carry His peaceful, gracious, hope-filled, faith-conquering nature.

You are emerging into a fuller personal relationship with His ways. You are becoming part of the answer for those who may, as yet, not have a clue how to live victoriously in ongoing chaos, disappointment, loss, grief, or disaster. You are gaining skills in mercy, giving, serving, and peace that pass all understanding and a miraculous expectation for God's grace and goodness. Your resilience is becoming a stronghold.

God wants to grant you vision for eternal significance. Our world is groaning for the appearance of people like you, the appearance of the true sons and daughters of God. That's you walking in the Spirit as a transformed transformer, expanding and exhibiting what the Kingdom of God is on the earth now (Romans 8:19). That Kingdom is more than numbers of people and gatherings of believers in churches with Sunday services. It is a real place where people live with His Kingdom nature expressed in and through their lives. That's God's Kingdom. It's where the King is not only in residence but ruling, where His character and ways are obvious.

You are being credited in heaven for each giving moment. You have the potential for tipping the scales for your nation. When all the nations come before our Lord as described in Matthew 25:31–34 (NKJV), there will be what the Bible describes as an eternal defining moment for each nation. Two groups will emerge: sheep and goats. And what are the deciding factors for each of them?

> "When the Son of Man comes in His glory, and all the holy angels with Him, then He will sit on the throne of His glory. All the nations will be

> gathered before Him, and He will separate them one from another, as a shepherd divides his sheep from the goats. And He will set the sheep on His right hand, but the goats on the left. Then the King will say to those on His right hand, "Come, you blessed of My Father, inherit the kingdom prepared for you from the foundation of the world."

The King then tells them why. How they treated the hungry, the poor, those without clothing, in prison or sick, were the deciding factors. In that list belong your parenting sacrifices.

The Son of Man then shares His loving heart for people by explaining that when they did any of these acts of kindness for anyone, no matter how small or unimportant this world may have labeled their efforts, they were being commended for ministering to the Lord Jesus Himself. Your Lord and Savior Jesus Christ considers what you do for others personally, as if you did them for Him.

As you have ministered to the least of these, He will say, you have done it to me. And now receive your reward: the Kingdom!

It's possible you could make the difference where your nation will stand on that day—on His right or on His left—a sheep or a goat nation. Individual acts equal corporate eternal blessing. Step by step, action by action, kindness builds, and God pays attention. You could be one of the people who tip the scales to the right with your continual serving your family and their special needs.

You are being transformed. It is becoming less and less difficult for you to embody His ways. The parenting royal adventure is well on its way. As you continue to fill your mind with His thoughts, you are growing in understanding and wisdom. As you do, His transforming power is renewing your mind (Romans 12:2). As your mind is being renewed, actions follow, and your positive influence becomes obvious. All kinds of unimaginable results occur. You live a Kingdom life. Your transformation is ongoing.

Philippians 3:20–21 says, "Our citizenship is in heaven. And we eagerly await a Savior from there, the Lord Jesus Christ, who, by the power that enables him to bring everything under his control, will transform our lowly bodies so that they will be like his glorious body."

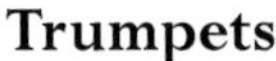

Trumpets

The trumpets of God, what did they say? My Jesus is coming,
so prepare the way.
When Jesus blew the trumpet, what was His chord?
I am the preparation and have come to be Lord.
What is the sound that we should now blow?
We declare the same-coming Jesus till at the last trump we go!

Revelation 11:15 says, "The seventh angel sounded his trumpet, and there were loud voices in heaven, which said: 'The kingdom of the world has become the kingdom of our Lord and of his Messiah, and he will reign for ever and ever.'"

Notes

Chapter 1

1. "As Long As I'm Here" from the album *As Long As I'm Here* copyright 2009, Independent. Ed and Roxanne Nilsen songs including the hit single "The Greatest Gift" as well as "This Side of Glory" are available to download on iTunes.
2. Therapist Faith Raimer, M.A., LMFT (www.faithhopeandtherapy.com). Faith is also a life coach, Christian counselor, speaker, and published author. Her Faith Hope and Therapy blog site is http://blog.faithhopeandtherapy.com.

Chapter 2

1. Caroline Leaf, PhD, *Who Switched Off My Brain? Controlling Toxic Thoughts and Emotions* (Improv, Ltd, 2009).
2. Joni Eareckson Tada, Joni and Friends, http://www.joniandfriends.org.
3. Nancy B. Miller, *Nobody's Perfect* (Baltimore, Maryland: Paul H. Brooks Publishing Co., 1994), 58.

Chapter 3

http://www.butterflymysteries.com/imaginal-cells.html.

Chapter 5

1. Nelson Mandela website https://www.nelsonmandela.org.
2. *Mandela: Long Walk to Freedom,* movie, 2013.
3. "Weird & Wild How Arctic Frogs Survive Being Frozen Alive" from voices.nationalgeographic.com Web post by Stefan Sirucek in Weird & Wild on August 21, 2013.

Chapter 6

1. Dr. Caroline Leaf, author of *Who Switched Off My Brain?* and *Switch On Your Brain*, Web post of May 23, 2014 (http://drleaf.com/blog/positive-versus-negative-stress/) and www.drleaf.net.
2. *Who Switched Off My Brain?* Kindle Version, distributed by Thomas Nelson Publishers 2009, 229, 558.
3. Nancy B. Miller, *Nobody's Perfect* (Baltimore, Maryland: Paul H. Brooks Publishing Co., 1994), 58.

Chapter 7

1. Shift Key definitions:
   http://www.webopedia.com/TERM/S/Shift_key.html.
   http://www.techterms.com/definition/shiftkey.
2. Laurie Vervaecke, *Woman Why Are You Weeping? Abuse: The Road to Recovery* (2009).

Chapter 8

1. James C. Dobson, *When God Doesn't Make Sense* (Tyndale House, 1993). Used by permission. Focus on the Family website http://www.focusonthe-family.com.

2. Rudyard Kipling, 1865–1936, was a British novelist and poet. His poem "If—" was first published in 1910 in a book of his poems, *Rewards and Fairies.*

Chapter 10

1. Melanie Boudreau, *Toppling the Idol of Ideal* (A Book's Mind, 2015), blog site MelanieBoudreau.com.
2. Cindy Steinbeck, *The Vine Speaks* (Concordia Publishing House, 2013).

Chapter 11

1. *Joyful Noiseletter* website http://www.joyfulnoiseletter.com.
2. Dawn McMullan, "The Happiness of Being Special" from *Live Happy* magazine.

Chapter 12

1. Susan Lana Hafner, *Though I Sleep, My Heart Is Awake* booklet (One Touch Publishing, 2008), 5-6, 12, onetouchawakening.org.
2. Susan Lana Hafner, *One Touch: The story of an Awakened Heart Expanded Edition with Discussion Guide by Susan Lana Hafner* (Creation House, 2013).

Chapter 14

1. Todd Burpo with Lynn Vincent, *Heaven is for Real: A Little Boy's Astounding Story of His Trip to Heaven and Back* (Thomas Nelson, 1999).
2. Website: www.godtube.com. Click on *Inspirational Videos.* In Search, type the names Quincy and Gracie Latkovski. You will watch a young girl gracefully dancing with her sister in a wheelchair.

More Books and Websites

Nancy B. Miller and Catherine C. Somons, *Everybody's Different* (Paul H. Brooks Publishing Co., 1999).

Amy Fenton Lee, *Leading a Special Needs Ministry* (Orange, a division of The re-think Group, Inc., 2013).

Ann Voskamp, *One Thousand Gifts* (Zondervon, 2010).

Stephanie O. Hubach, *Same Lake Different Boat* (P & R Publishing, 2006).

Phil Whitehead, *Thriving in the Grace of God* (Sovereign World Ltd., 2004).

Louie Giglio, *How Great is our God – Laminin* www.youtube.com/watch?v= iCrvibgo1LM.

Jane Hansen Hoyt, *Master Plan* (Aglow International, 2009) aglow.org.

Jane Hansen Hoyt, *The View From Above, Living Life From God's Perspective* (Aglow International, 2011) aglow.org.

Phil Hansen, speaker, *Embrace the Shake,* TED Talks, ted.com.

Joni Eareckson Tada, *Pearls of Great Price* (Zondervan, 2006).

About the Author

Melonie Janet Mangum is a skilled people person, lovingly involved in the lives of countless people. As a young woman, she worked at her local school district in the Special Education department. The connection she made there with the parents of children with special needs challenged her to do more. In response, she pioneered the Touchpoint for Parents group at her local church.

An ordained minister, she earned her practical theology doctorate degree with an emphasis in Christian education and evangelism in 1995 and her doctorate of theology degree (ThD) in 1998 from International College of Bible Theology.

Since 1992 Melonie has worked with teams of all ages, both developing the team members as well as leading teams that train and equip people in numerous nations around the world. She is the founder and president of Partners For Transformation (partners4transformation.com). She also serves Aglow International as the Transformation Director (Aglow.org). She is the loving mother of three and grandmother living in Newbury Park, California.

YOUR THOUGHTS

51360034R00133

Made in the USA
San Bernardino, CA
20 July 2017